Department of International Economic and Social A

Chawla, Sandeep.

THE SITUATION
OF YOUTH IN THE 1980s
AND
PROSPECTS
AND CHALLENGES
FOR THE YEAR 2000

UNITED NATIONS

New York, 1986

NOTE

The designations employed and the presentation of the material in this publication do not imply the expression of any opinion whatsoever on the part of the Secretariat of the United Nations concerning the legal status of any country, territory, city or area or of its authorities, or concerning the delimitation of its frontiers or boundaries.

Material in this publication may be freely quoted or reprinted, but acknowledgement is requested, together with a copy of the publication containing the quotation or reprint.

ST/ESA/186

UNITED NATIONS PUBLICATION
Sales No. E.86.IV.10
ISBN 92-1-130117-3
01100P

PREFACE

The present sales publication has been prepared for the United Nations in accordance with the proposed programme budget for the 1984-1985 biennium, subprogramme element 6.2, "Youth policies and programmes". Based upon extensive data, from both within and without the United Nations system, the study reviews the global situation of youth in the 1980s and examines the prospects for young people in the year 2000.

It is hoped that this publication will contribute to the attainment of the objectives of the International Youth Year: Participation, Development, Peace (1985).

This study was prepared by Dr. Sandeep Chawla, a consultant with the United Nations Secretariat.

CONTENTS

Tables

Explanatory notes

References to dollars ($) are to United States dollars unless otherwise stated.

A full stop is used to indicate decimals.

A comma is used to distinguish thousands and millions.

The term "billion" signifies a thousand million.

The following symbols have been used in tables:

Three dots (...) indicate that data are not available or are not separately reported.

A dash (-) indicates that the amount is nil or negligible.

A blank indicates that the item is not applicable.

A minus sign before a figure (-2) denotes a deficit or decrease, except as otherwise indicated.

An asterisk (*) indicates provisional or estimated figures.

The following abbreviations have been used:

GDP gross domestic product
GNP gross national product
NMP net material product
HYV high-yielding variety

The designations employed and the presentation of the material in this publication do not imply the expression of any opinion whatsoever on the part of the Secretariat of the United Nations concerning the legal status of any country or territory or of its authorities, or concerning the delimitation of its frontiers.

The term "country" as used in the text of this report also refers, as appropriate, to territories or areas.

For analytical purposes, the following country classification has been used:

Centrally planned economies: China, Eastern Europe and Union of Soviet Socialist Republics

Developed market economies: North America, southern and western Europe (excluding Cyprus, Malta and Yugoslavia), Australia, Japan, New Zealand and South Africa

Developing countries: Latin America and the Caribbean area, Africa (other than South Africa), Asia (excluding Japan) and Cyprus, Malta and Yugoslavia

More developed countries/regions/areas: Covers centrally planned
economies and developed
market economies

Less developed countries/regions/areas: Covers developing
countries and areas

The designations of country groups in the text and the tables are intended solely for statistical or analytical convenience and do not necessarily express a judgement about the stage reached by a particular country or area in the development process.

I. THE CONCEPTION OF YOUTH: GENERAL CONSIDERATIONS

The evolution of the conception

In the world at large, every day that passes claims the lives of 40,000 children. 1/ Every month that has passed in the 40 years since the end of the Second World War has claimed an average of 37,000 violent deaths as a result of armed conflicts - conflicts which, ipso facto, decimate more younger than older people. 2/ This, while it may appear to some as a terrifying Malthusian dénouement, is an implacable reality of the world at the mid-point of the 1980s. So many children dying every day would seem to imply that the age structure of the global population should move more in favour of older generations. Yet, this implication is belied by the fact that the global youth population has been growing continuously since 1950, was estimated to be 922 million in 1984, and is projected to cross the 1,000 million mark towards the end of the decade. What kind of world do these young people encounter? Youth unemployment figures are currently approaching 50 per cent in both developed and developing countries, excluding socialist countries. 3/ Across a complex spectrum of regional, national and local diversity, a myriad of other compelling problems confront young people.

In the present study, an effort is made to provide a conspectus of the situation of youth in the 1980s and the prospects for young people in the year 2000. The rationale for a work of this nature is manifest in the fact that at present one of every five inhabitants in the world happens to be a youth - defined by the United Nations as a person between 15 and 24 years of age. In 1984, the estimated youth population of 922 million constituted 19.4 per cent of the total global population. The demographic significance of this, which is detailed below, is, of course, a factor of the more general social significance of youth. What exactly constitutes this significance is difficult to measure, though there has been considerable progress in this regard.

The hinge of the issue is what exactly "youth" means. The explanatory power and universal applicability of most rigorous definitions tend to break down in the face of two different sets of factors. In the first place is the very considerable variety in how different societies conceive of youth. In the second place is the fact that definitions of youth, based upon such conceptions, change continuously, as a response to a perpetually changing social and economic milieu. Because the social and economic situation of any particular society varies from one historical moment to another, it follows that there will be a commensurate variation, spatial as well as temporal, in that society's conceptions and definitions of youth. While common denominators can doubtless be found, it is important to consider, albeit briefly, the operation of these two sets of factors in the evolution of a general conception of youth.

In some traditional societies, youth, either as a notion or a social reality, did not exist. 4/ There was no hiatus - what we now refer to as a "generation gap" - between childhood and adulthood. Occupational choice was seldom a problem; vocational training, though usually by rote, was an integral part of the social structure. There was thus little of the apparent contra- diction that is inherent in the modern conception of youth: persons whom society ceases to regard as children, yet does not regard as full adults. This modern conception often became social fact as a result of traditional social formations becoming more modernized and complex. Learning by rote was not nearly enough; work became technologically more complex; specialized skills had to be acquired in order to integrate into the occupational structure; the age of maturity moved upwards. The hiatus between childhood and adulthood consequently became socially necessary.

While this does not apply across the board to all traditional societies, there are still comparable situations, even in the present. Many children in some of the less developed regions of the world are never even given the luxury of being "young". Global estimates made by the International Labour Organisation show that there are some 50 million children under the age of 15 who are at work. Of the 10 to 14 age group, 11 per cent are economically active. Nearly 98 per cent of all these child labourers are found in developing countries. 5/ The striking increase in the urban youth populations of less developed regions 6/ has created the phenomenon of the "street children": children who live and work on the streets, doing anything that will earn them and their families that little extra which enables them to survive. In 1983, an international conference in New York estimated that there were 70 to 90 million abandoned street children in the world. 7/ More recent estimates by the United Nations Children's Fund, based upon global interpolations of country studies, suggest that these figures were gross underestimations, and that the realistic figure would be a global population of 170 million, which constitutes a startling 3.8 per cent of the total world population. 7/ If "youth" is understood as constituting the period between the end of childhood, on the one hand, and entry into the world of work, on the other, then it is manifest that youth does not exist in the situations outlined above.

It would appear, then, that a certain paradigm of modern industrialized society has engendered a world-view which equates the ages of formal secondary and higher education with youth, or with the transition from childhood to adulthood. Particularly in the 1960s, many of the studies on youth were predicated upon such an assumption. 8/ The provenance of these studies - Western Europe, North America, and some major cities in Asia and Latin America - is also indicative of the areas in which this modern conception of youth evolved and received plaudits. Its parameters, however, were limited. Youth meant young people who were primarily urban, middle-class and at university. The parameters stopped short of considering many young people who were rural, uneducated, under-privileged and apparently inarticulate. Much valuable research was nevertheless done. A great deal of this was concentrated upon trying to comprehend the intermediate period between childhood and adulthood - a period necessitated by rapid technological and economic change, which often made it desirable for each generation to be trained to work and act differently from the way its parents did. The results of this research contributed to the tendency to perceive youth problems as problems of deviance or deprivation, and youth as a potential source of social change.

The role that young people could play in the process of social change was articulated in the West European and North American youth movements during the late 1960s. The parameters of the existing conception of youth had to be widened in order to take cognizance of these relatively new assertions of specific identity and interest. Among the many dimensions of youth and student protest in this period, one which is significant in this context is the scepticism towards traditional institutions in modern society, such as the university, and the search for alternative forms of social participation, 9/ such as the primordial symbolism of direct social participation embodied in the "hippie" movement. The outcome of these protest movements reflects the fact that they embodied no coherent and workable alternatives to the institutions and structures they were protesting against. 9/ Reforms, however, did follow, some of them embodying the foci of the youth movements. Inherent in this process of reform was the continued growth of the general conception of youth,

as it had to incorporate all these variegated changes. Perhaps the most
crucial change was the increasing recognition that there was a basic solidarity
among the youth of the world at large. This meant that various sub-categories
of youth, such as rural or uneducated youth, began to acquire more social
recognition than they had hitherto received.

One of the defining characteristics of the global milieu in the late 1960s
was the almost universal belief that economic growth was, and would continue to
be, a constant. Particularly in the more developed regions of the world, ever-
increasing material abundance began to be thought of as a permanent reality;
scarcity as something that was unlikely to recur. The concern, therefore, was
more with questions of the cultural and attitudinal reflections of this apparent
prosperity. While doubts may have been raised about the distribution of wealth
and income, the fact of continued abundance was seldom questioned. The youth
movements of course acted within this climate of opinion, and even the apparent
austerity of the hippie communal "counter culture" was predicated upon the
expectation of an always prosperous society that could afford to support people
who even rejected its basic occupational structure.

This assessment of the climate of opinion in the more developed regions
must be conflated with the situation in the less developed regions of the world.
Here too, the late 1960s were a period of general optimism about prosperity and
stability in the international economic system. The optimism was reflected in
the programme for the first United Nations Development Decade (1960s). 10/
While the majority of developing countries faced enormous problems, these
problems were generally regarded as surmountable, particularly in the light of
an apparent solidarity in the international system. As decolonization reached
its culmination, the key issue became that of development. In the burgeoning of
development plans and activities that followed, youth was frequently considered
a major asset whose energies could be positively harnessed. Many young people
became involved in this process, and in the corollary one of asserting their own
specific identity. Here was fertile ground for ideas that often originated in
the milieu and youth movements of Europe and North America. A certain unified
concept of youth, informed by these many facets of different situations around
the world, began to emerge.

More severe changes were yet to come. The early 1970s saw the evanescence
of optimism as the bubble of ever-increasing material abundance burst. Recession
and scarcity began to jeopardize faith in the inevitability of economic progress.
In a response typical of hard times, social groups closed their ranks; so, often,
did societies in general. These tendencies transposed themselves into the international environment, often giving it a tenebrous character. As the 1970s
unfolded, it became increasingly apparent that the economic crisis was not merely
a transient phenomenon. While there was some evidence of an apparent recovery,
the early 1980s saw another sharp recession. Economic uncertainty, scarcity and
deprivation began to be recognized as phenomena which characterized the 1970s,
and plausibly the 1980s as well. The contrast with the 1960s is apparent: the
one was a crisis primarily of culture, of ideas, of institutions; the other (the
1970s and early 1980s) a more concrete structural crisis that made inflation and
unemployment household words, and rules rather than exceptions. While this
situation prevailed, in the main, in the market economies of the world, the
centrally planned economies were not entirely unaffected. Bedevilled by problems
of their own, which will be detailed below, they faced the consequences of the
international tension and uncertainty that are usually a concomitant of economic
crises.

These events had immense consequences, both for the real situation of young people all over the world and for the still evolving conception of youth. The former will be analysed below, since it constitutes the major concern of this study. For the latter, it is important to note that it was these events of the 1970s and early 1980s that set an indistinguishable impression upon our contemporary concept of youth. The relatively narrow and arguably optimistic conception of the 1960s gave way to the more realistic, rigorous and wider conception of the present, a result of the conflation of social reality with a specific social group's perception of it. Youth was no more what other, mostly older, people wanted it to be. It was what young people themselves saw, felt and asserted it to be. What a majority of them experienced was a certain difficulty in the process of making the transition from childhood to adulthood. This difficulty, experienced to a greater or lesser degree, became a demonstrably generalized phenomenon, although it had specific and unique regional, national and local manifestations. 11/

The process of "growing up", then, came to be recognized as one that was frequently complicated by a variety of problems: difficulties in education, cultural transmission, employment, social integration and participation, health, housing, and development in general. These problems, among others, will be examined below, as they are determinants of the situation of youth. But they are also important in this connection, since they now inform our conception of youth. For many young people in the world, there is no stage of "youth" at all; for others, it is precariously short and tenuous; for still others, it is indefinitely prolonged. Poverty, deprivation, scarcity, uncertainty - all these are things which many young people must square with, in economic, social and psychological terms. In the less developed parts of the world, many young people begin to work even before they enter their teens. In the more developed regions of the world, many young people find it difficult to acquire the socially accepted status of adulthood because they cannot find jobs. Between these two extremes, there is a complex variety of situations and cases, and a valid conception of youth must encompass the majority, if not all, of them.

The conception

How, then, do we view this conception? Youth should be seen as both a product of social reproduction and a force for social change or transformation. These two roles could be independent of each other, such as young people cleaving to reproductive activities by replicating patterns of older generations, or pursuing a path of social transformation by participating in movements for social change. The two roles could also be pursued simultaneously, a result of the young people in question differentiating between what they accept, and what they wish to change, in a given social milieu. This duality should be balanced with another one. If youth is conceived of as an age category, then it should be properly sub-divided into two sub-categories: adolescents and young adults. Adolescence is generally regarded as the period during which society ceases to regard the individual as a child, but does not yet accord him the full status, roles and functions of adulthood. 12/ Young adulthood is a step beyond, but still does not constitute full adult status with the access to the various family, professional and political rights which this implies, and usually confers.

Youth is not a biological notion, as, for instance, puberty is. It is, rather, a sociological concept: an attitudinal system and a behavioural pattern related to a specific position in society. This is not to deny the relationship between sociological and biological forces, but merely to distinguish them. Any age category - for instance childhood, youth, or old age - is predicated upon

biological facts, yet is structured by social forces. It is this process of
socialization that is so different, spatially as well as temporally, since the
social forces in question vary from moment to moment as well as from one
society to another. Yet, differences notwithstanding, the very fact of
socialization, upon a given biological group, gives rise to a set of partially
shared perceptions and problems, which, among other things, contribute to the
creation of a common identity. "Youth" is the generic notion used to describe
this common identity. Since a variety of diverse social forces structure the
youth of a particular society, it follows that the social roles of the young
people in question will be contingent upon the specific configurations of these
forces. The social role itself, as noted above, is best understood in terms of
the dual reproductive and transformative functions that characterize youth in
any society. It is these configurations of social forces, and the various
roles of youth which they engender, that this study seeks to examine: the
situation of youth in the present and in the near future, and the prospects
and challenges for the year 2000.

The 15-24 definition, despite some limitations, offers a certain
statistical utility, as well as the practical convenience of a definite
analytical tool for examining a complex web of regional and national
differences. It is based upon the recognition that youth, despite the
heterogeneity of its components, constitutes a social group with its own
specific identity, needs, problems and cultural configurations, as well as
the actual articulation of these things by young people in many different
parts of the world. The definition, in order to be used effectively, must be
interpreted in as flexible a manner as possible. Both the upper and the lower
limits of the age bracket need not be rigidly adhered to, except of course in
purely statistical exercises.

One major reason for downward flexibility in the age bracket has been
noted already: the global phenomenon of children who are in the work force.
An equally compelling reason for upward flexibility in the age bracket is the
other global phenomenon of youth unemployment. Many young people have
difficulty in finding work, and are therefore unable to lead an independent
family life. In traditional societies, there were usually some initiation
rites whereby full adult status was conferred upon a certain individual.
Modern societies have no such initiation rites, but various critical events
are characteristic of the status of adulthood. Two of the most obvious and
common such events are marriage and entry into an occupation. If these two
events are taken as indicators of full adult status, then a person who has
neither indicator could continue to be considered a youth, even if he were
over 25 years of age. Flexibility is thus important in this context, and as
long as it is applied, the 15-24 age bracket appears to be a valid and useful
common denominator.

International Youth Year

In recent years, it has become something of a platitude to say that young
people are particularly vulnerable to the effects of the global social and
economic crisis. Equally commonplace is another formulation related to this:
that young people must be effectively integrated into the process of development in order to overcome the global crisis and its regional, national and
local manifestations. The validity of these positions is as unquestionable as
it is demonstrably important. However, there is little unanimity on how
exactly these things should be done - on how the mechanics of young people's
participation, in development in particular, and in society in general, should
be facilitated. In the various solutions adopted, there is considerable
regional and national diversity. Moreover, there has been a general tendency

towards fragmentation in identifying, conceptualizing, and attempting
solutions to, the specific problems of young people.

The International Youth Year (1985) was an attempt to end this
fragmentation. The concept of youth has now become very much a part of
international discourse, and the international community has invested
considerable effort in coming to grips with the many problems that young
people face, as well as in attempting to ensure that the vast potential for
development that young people so clearly have is effectively harnessed.
International concern has developed into consensus, and the decade of the
1980s is crucial in this respect. Thus, the International Development
Strategy for the Third United Nations Development Decade recommends that all
countries give high priority to the mobilization and integration of youth in
development. 13/ The focus of these general development plans sharpened in
the designation of 1985 as International Youth Year. 14/

The Year, as it was conceived, was, ipso facto, a unique event. Preparations for it had been under way since 1980. Built into its mechanisms was a
planning period during which Governments, non-governmental organizations, youth
organizations and the United Nations system assessed the situation of youth,
and, upon this basis, proposed medium- and long-term measures to solve the
problems of youth. Unlike other special events, the Year had a specific
programme of measures and activities which was formulated prior to it, in
1981. 15/ This programme provided a framework of activities to be undertaken
prior to the Year itself, as preparatory measures. There already existed,
therefore, well before 1985, the broad contours of a common global strategy on
youth. There were also several mechanisms to give weight and direction to this
strategy, among them an International Youth Year Trust Fund. Five regional
assessments of the situation of youth, presented to five regional meetings
devoted to the Year, in 1983, 16/ formed the bases for five regional plans of
action on youth. 17/ All this information and experience was subsequently
integrated into two major avenues: the preparation of the present study, and,
in conjunction with this, detailed guidelines for further planning and suitable
follow-up in the field of youth. 18/ These would thus serve as analytical
tools and an empirical basis for refining the conceptual parameters of the Year
as well as for strengthening the pragmatic utility of its three concurrent
frameworks: (a) thematic: participation, development, peace; (b) temporal:
before, during and after 1985; and (c) spatial: the international, regional
and national levels. Consequently, 1985 was not the sum total of the
International Youth Year. It was, rather, the hinge of a continuum which spans
the decade, and which, it is hoped, will go even beyond.

Notes

1/ United Nations Children's Fund, The State of the World's Children, 1984
(New York, Oxford University Press, 1984), p. 5.

2/ 1985 Report on the World Social Situation" (United Nations publication,
Sales No. E/CN.5/1985/2, E.85.IV.2); "General and complete disarmament: study on
conventional disarmament - Report of the Secretary-General" (A/39/348,
31 August 1984); and Ruth Leger Sivard, World Military and Social Expenditures, 1983
(Washington, D.C., World Priorities, 1983), p. 21.

3/ United Nations press release (ILO/2189), 16 November 1984.

4/ See Margaret Mead, Coming of Age in Samoa (New York, 1949) and United
Nations Educational, Scientific and Cultural Organization, New Approaches to Rural
Youth and Development in Latin America and the Caribbean (Paris, 1981), pp. 12-13.

5/ "Rural youth in the less developed countries", Note by the secretariat of the United Nations Food and Agriculture Organization, 31 July 1984.

6/ See tables 4 and 5.

7/ United Nations Children's Fund, Ideas Forum, Nos. 18 and 19, 1984/3 and 4.

8/ See the detailed bibliography in L. Rosenmayr and K. Allerbeck, "Youth and society", special issue of Current Sociology, vol. 27, No. 2/3 (1979), pp. 153-335.

9/ S. N. Eisenstadt, "Cultural settings and adolescence and youth around the year 2000", in Adolescence and Youth in Prospect, J. P. Hill and F. J. Monks, eds. (Dorking, 1977), pp. 114-24; and R. G. Braungart, "Youth and social movements", in Adolescence in the Life Cycle, S. Dragastin and G. Elder, eds. (Washington, D.C., 1975), pp. 255-289.

10/ General Assembly resolution 1710 (XVI).

11/ United Nations Educational, Scientific and Cultural Organization, Conférence Internationale sur la Jeunesse, 1964: Final Report (Paris, 1964); "Report of the Secretary-General on the situation of youth" (E/CN.5/486, 1972); 1974 Report on the World Social Situation (United Nations publication, Sales No. E.75.IV.6), pp. 247-50; and "Report of the Secretary-General on problems confronting youth and the manner in which these problems are being treated by organs and executive bodies of the United Nations system" (E/CN.5/534, 1976).

12/ See A. B. Hollingshead, Elmtown's Youth: The Impact of Social Classes on Adolescents (New York, 1961), p. 6.

13/ General Assembly resolution 35/56.

14/ General Assembly resolution 34/151.

15/ A/36/215.

16/ "The situation of youth in the Asian and Pacific Region" (SD/RPMIYY/1, 19 May 1983), paper presented to the Regional Preparatory Meeting for the International Youth Year, Bangkok, 26-30 July 1983; "The situation of youth in Europe" (IYY/ECE/RPM/2, 24 June 1983), paper presented to the Regional Preparatory Meeting on International Youth Year, Costinesti, 5-9 September 1983; "The situation and prospects of youth in Latin America" (E/CEPAL/CONF.75/L.2, 5 September 1983), paper presented to the Regional Preparatory Meeting on International Youth Year, San Jose, 3-7 October 1983; "The situation and needs of youth in Western Asia" (E/ECWA/SDP/W.G.I./3, 1 August 1983), paper presented to the Regional Preparatory Meeting on International Youth Year, Baghdad, 9-13 October 1983.

17/ International Youth Year: Regional Plans of Action, 1983 (United Nations publication, 1984).

18/ A/40/256.

II. DEMOGRAPHIC PROFILE*

The world youth population and its growth

The world youth population was estimated to be 922 million in 1984 (table 1). This represented a 79 per cent increase from the 515 million in 1960 and a 39 per cent increase from the 661 million in 1970. The size of the 15-24 age group is projected to exceed 1,000 million towards the end of the 1980s and to increase to 1,062 million in 2000 and 1,309 million in 2025 (table 2).

Although the world youth population has been growing continuously since 1950, the annual rate of growth has changed considerably. It rose sharply from 0.8 per cent in 1955-1960 to 3.2 per cent in 1965-1970. Since then it has declined gradually, to 2.0 per cent in the first half of the 1980s. This downward trend is projected to continue, with a sharp drop to 0.4 per cent in the 1990s.

Table 1. Youth population in 1984

Region/country	Both sexes	Male	Female	Both sexes
		(thousands)		(percentage)
World	921 772	469 639	452 134	19.4
More developed regions	187 283	95 560	91 722	16.5
Less developed regions	734 489	374 079	360 412	20.4
Africa	102 197	51 249	50 949	19.0
Latin America	80 400	40 525	39 875	20.2
North America	44 879	22 789	22 090	17.2
East Asia	255 773	130 547	125 227	20.6
South Asia	311 912	159 830	152 082	20.3
Europe	76 829	39 335	37 494	15.7
Oceania	4 368	2 241	2 127	17.9
USSR	45 413	23 123	22 290	16.5

Source: Department of International Economic and Social Affairs of the United Nations Secretariat.

The size of the global youth population is determined by two factors: the number of births 15 to 24 years before, which is a function of the number of women at childbearing ages and their fertility, and the rate of survival from birth to the age group in question. The improvement in survival rate has a substantial impact on the increase of youth population. For example, although the average annual growth rate of the youth population was 2.1 per cent in 1975-1984 and is projected to be 0.9 per cent in 1984-2000, it would be 1.2 and 0.4 per cent in the respective periods if there were no mortality decline. The impact of mortality improvement on the youth population growth, however, changes

---

*This chapter is based on a paper prepared by the Population Division, Department of International Economic and Social Affairs, entitled "Demographic situation and prospects of the youth population", 8 August 1984.

Table 2. Youth population, 1950-2025

Youth population	1950	1960	1970	1980	1985	1990	2000	2025
World								
Thousands	463 958	514 659	661 003	849 536	940 368	1 022 147	1 061 519	1 308 560
Growth rate (percentage) a/	-	0.8	3.2	2.1	2.0	1.7	0.4	0.3
Percentage of total population	18.5	17.1	17.9	19.1	19.4	19.5	17.3	16.0
More developed regions								
Thousands	142 928	144 002	174 799	192 060	185 947	177 027	173 990	179 158
Growth rate (percentage) a/	-	-0.1	2.5	-0.6	0.6	-1.0	0.1	0.1
Percentage of total population	17.2	15.2	16.7	16.9	15.9	14.7	13.7	12.9
Less developed regions								
Thousands	321 029	370 657	486 203	657 476	754 420	845 120	887 529	1 129 402
Growth rate (percentage) a/	-	1.2	3.5	2.5	2.8	2.3	0.4	0.3
Percentage of total population	19.2	17.9	18.4	19.8	20.6	20.9	18.3	16.7
Africa								
Thousands	41 545	51 634	65 692	90 235	105 461	122 040	170 069	341 263
Growth rate (percentage) a/	-	2.2	2.6	3.3	3.1	2.9	3.4	2.1
Percentage of total population	18.7	18.6	18.4	19.0	19.1	18.9	19.4	20.8
Latin America								
Thousands	31 325	38 686	53 572	73 673	82 138	88 858	104 817	128 949
Growth rate (percentage) a/	-	2.2	3.6	3.0	2.2	1.6	1.7	0.5
Percentage of total population	19.0	17.8	18.9	20.3	20.2	19.6	19.1	16.4
North America								
Thousands	24 553	27 197	40 483	47 546	44 159	39 491	40 526	44 773
Growth rate (percentage) a/	-	2.5	3.5	1.0	-1.5	-2.2	1.2	0.4
Percentage of total population	14.8	13.7	17.9	18.9	16.8	14.3	13.6	12.9

continued

Table 2 (continued)

	1950	1960	1970	1980	1985	1990	2000	2025
East Asia								
Thousands	130 340	135 692	183 047	225 652	263 426	300 081	219 385	226 086
Growth rate (percentage) a/	-	-0.1	4.4	1.0	3.1	2.6	-3.8	-1.6
Percentage of total population	19.4	16.9	18.6	19.1	21.0	22.8	14.9	13.3
South Asia								
Thousands	133 729	161 815	202 983	282 916	319 372	351 695	407 501	446 742
Growth rate (percentage) a/	-	1.7	2.7	3.2	2.4	1.9	1.4	-0.1
Percentage of total population	19.2	18.7	18.3	20.1	20.3	20.2	19.7	16.1
Europe								
Thousands	63 304	62 400	71 405	76 280	76 952	74 136	66 974	63 786
Growth rate (percentage) a/	-	-0.2	1.4	0.4	0.2	-0.8	-0.7	-0.3
Percentage of total population	16.2	14.7	15.5	15.8	15.7	14.9	13.1	12.2
Oceania								
Thousands	1 961	2 364	3 426	4 199	4 409	4 565	4 850	5 814
Growth rate (percentage) a/	-	3.0	3.2	2.0	1.0	0.7	0.7	0.6
Percentage of total population	15.5	15.0	17.7	18.2	17.8	17.1	16.0	14.7
USSR								
Thousands	37 199	34 871	40 395	49 036	44 449	41 482	47 396	51 148
Growth rate (percentage) a/	-	-2.3	4.9	1.0	-2.0	-1.5	1.6	0.6
Percentage of total population	20.7	16.3	16.7	18.5	16.0	14.2	15.2	13.9

Source: Department of International Economic and Social Affairs of the United Nations Secretariat.

a/ The growth rate refers to the average annual rate of increase for each five-year period preceding the given year.

gradually over time, so that rises and falls in the growth rate of the 15-24 age
group that occurred and will occur in the second half of the century are, to a
greater extent, a reflection of fluctuation in the rate of births.

The low growth rate of the youth population in the late 1950s is likely
to have reflected the slow increase of births during the Second World War.
The number of births grew very rapidly in the post-war decade of 1945-1955,
resulting in a large proportional increase of youth population around the year
1970.

The growth rate of births fluctuated around 1960 as a combined result of
two counteracting factors: the rapidly increasing number of women at
childbearing ages and the moderate pace of fertility reduction. Then the
growth rate of births decreased significantly to a trough of -0.6 per cent in
the mid-1970s, resulting mainly from accelerated fertility reduction in less
developed regions. It should be noted that most women born in the post-war
decade reached the peak ages of childbearing in the 1970s, so that they could
have produced a large increase of births. These women, however, exhibited a
significantly lower fertility than their preceding generations.

This trend of decreasing births from the 1950s to the 1970s, with a slow
decline in the early years and a sharp drop at the end, is reflected in the
growth rate of the youth population from the 1970s to the 1990s, which is
marked with a current gradual decline that will be followed by a steep fall in
the last decade of the century. Despite this fall, the absolute number of
young people will still be considerable, and will constitute 17.3 per cent of
the total global population in the year 2000.

Youth population in the major regions of the world

In 1984, some 187 million young people lived in more developed regions and
734 million lived in less developed regions. Thus, four out of five young
people are residents of less developed regions. The difference in the relative
size of the youth population between these regions is increasing, owing to the
differential growth rates of the 15-24 group in the two regions. In 1984, the
less developed regions accounted for 76 per cent of the total global population.
The youth component of the population of these regions rose from 69 per cent of
the total global population in 1950 to 74 per cent in 1970 and 80 per cent in
1984, and will be 84 per cent in the year 2000.

The distribution of youth population among the major regions of the world
in 1984 was as follows: Asia had the largest share (more than 60 per cent), as
South Asia constituted 34 per cent and East Asia 28 per cent of the world youth
population; following Asia were, in decreasing order, Africa (11 per cent),
Latin America (9 per cent), Europe (8 per cent), North America (5 per cent),
USSR (5 per cent) and Oceania (0.5 per cent).

The youth population in these regions is growing at considerably different
rates. Between 1970 and 1984, the average annual growth rate of the 15-24 group
was the highest in Africa (3.2 per cent) and South Asia (3.1 per cent), followed
by Latin America (2.9 per cent), East Asia (2.4 per cent) and Oceania (1.7 per
cent). The growth rate was below 1 per cent in the USSR (0.8 per cent), North
America (0.7 per cent) and Europe (0.5 per cent).

The regional variation in youth population growth will be somewhat different
in the near future. The average annual growth rate from 1984 to 2000 will remain
at a very high level in Africa (3.2 per cent). By contrast, the rate of
increase in East Asia will fall very sharply, to the negative annual growth of

-1.0 per cent, resulting mainly from the fertility decline in China in the recent past. The other regions will also experience a decline, although it will not be as steep as that in East Asia. The average rate of increase from 1984 to 2000 will be relatively high in Latin America (1.7 per cent) and South Asia (1.7 per cent), though quite low in Oceania (0.7 per cent), USSR (0.3 per cent), North America (-0.6 per cent) and Europe (-0.9 per cent).

These differential growth rates of the youth population in major regions introduce significant changes in the regional distribution of young people. As seen in table 3, the share of the world youth population increased between 1970 and 1984 in Africa, Latin America and South Asia, remained constant in East Asia and Oceania, and decreased in North America, Europe and the USSR. These trends are projected to continue in 1984-2000, except that Africa's share will increase at a considerably more rapid pace than before, and the share of East Asia will exhibit a sharp downturn.

Table 3. World youth population, major regions, 1950-2000
(Percentage)

Region/country	1950	1970	1984	2000
More developed regions	30.8	26.4	20.3	16.4
Less developed regions	69.2	73.6	79.7	83.6
Africa	9.0	9.9	11.1	16.0
Latin America	6.8	8.1	8.7	9.9
North America	5.3	6.1	4.9	3.8
East Asia	28.1	27.7	27.7	20.7
South Asia	28.8	30.7	33.8	38.4
Europe	13.6	10.8	8.3	6.3
Oceania	0.4	0.5	0.5	0.5
USSR	8.0	6.1	4.9	4.5

Source: Department of International Economic and Social Affairs of the United Nations Secretariat.

Youth population in urban and rural areas*

Of the 922 million young people in the world in 1984, some 410 million (44 per cent) lived in urban areas and 512 million (56 per cent) in rural areas. Thus, approximately 9 out of 20 young people are urban residents. For a variety of social reasons, young people are more likely to live in urban areas than the rest of the population. The proportion of the world population living in urban areas was 41 per cent for all ages combined in 1984, somewhat lower than the percentage for youth. This tendency is observed in both more developed regions

---

*This section is based on the latest estimates and projections of age and sex structure of urban and rural populations prepared by the Population Division, as presented in "Age and sex structure of urban and rural populations, 1970-2000: the 1980 assessment" (ESA/P/WP.81), with some minor adjustments in light of the Population Division's 1982 assessment of demographic estimates and projections.

(78 per cent for youth versus 72 per cent for the total) and less developed regions (36 per cent for youth versus 31 per cent for the total). Such tendencies are considered a reflection of the migration of young people from rural to urban areas for employment, education and other opportunities.

The proportion of young people residing in urban areas differs significantly among major regions of the world, as shown in table 4. It was 78 per cent in more developed regions in 1984, considerably higher than the 36 per cent in less developed regions. The highest proportion was observed in the USSR (81 per cent) and North America (80 per cent), followed by Oceania (79 per cent) and Europe (74 per cent). On the other hand, fewer than half of the young people were urban residents in Africa (36 per cent), East Asia (35 per cent) and South Asia (30 per cent) in 1984. Among the less developed regions, Latin America has a relatively high proportion of urban residents (70 per cent).

Table 4. Urban and rural youth population,
world and regions, 1970-2000

Youth population	1970	1984	2000
World			
Urban (thousands)	264 838	409 932	565 219
Rural (thousands)	396 166	511 840	496 300
Urban (percentage)	40.1	44.5	53.2
More developed regions			
Urban (thousands)	125 256	145 927	145 406
Rural (thousands)	49 543	41 356	28 583
Urban (percentage)	71.7	77.9	83.6
Less developed regions			
Urban (thousands)	139 582	264 005	419 813
Rural (thousands)	346 623	470 484	467 717
Urban (percentage)	28.7	35.9	47.3
Africa			
Urban (thousands)	17 225	36 689	80 672
Rural (thousands)	48 467	65 508	89 397
Urban (percentage)	26.2	35.9	47.4
Latin America			
Urban (thousands)	31 880	55 976	80 944
Rural (thousands)	21 692	24 424	23 873
Urban (percentage)	59.5	69.6	77.2
North America			
Urban (thousands)	30 749	35 972	34 247
Rural (thousands)	9 744	8 908	6 279
Urban (percentage)	75.9	80.2	84.5

continued

Table 4 (continued)

Youth population	1970	1984	2000
East Asia			
Urban (thousands)	54 730	89 827	102 126
Rural (thousands)	128 317	165 946	117 260
Urban (percentage)	29.9	35.1	46.6
South Asia			
Urban (thousands)	50 136	94 908	169 016
Rural (thousands)	152 847	217 004	238 484
Urban (percentage)	24.7	30.4	41.5
Europe			
Urban (thousands)	47 462	56 530	52 943
Rural (thousands)	23 944	20 299	14 032
Urban (percentage)	66.5	73.6	79.0
Oceania			
Urban (thousands)	2 455	3 428	4 005
Rural (thousands)	971	940	845
Urban (percentage)	71.7	78.5	82.6
USSR			
Urban (thousands)	30 298	36 602	41 265
Rural (thousands)	10 187	8 811	6 131
Urban (percentage)	74.8	80.6	87.1

Source: Department of International Economic and Social Affairs of the United Nations Secretariat.

Demographic trends in the youth population are substantially different in urban and rural areas. The increase in the urban youth population the world over has been significantly higher than the increase in the rural youth population. From 1970 to 1984, the world urban youth population grew at an average annual rate of 3.1 per cent, and is projected to continue growing at 2.0 per cent between 1984 and 2000 (see table 5). The comparable average annual growth rates for the world rural youth population were 1.8 per cent between 1970 and 1984, and a projected decline of 0.2 per cent from 1984 to 2000. In particular, the number of rural youth decreased in North America, Europe, Oceania and the USSR. As a result of the differential growth of urban and rural youth populations, the proportion of youth living in urban areas in the world increased from 40 per cent in 1970 to 44 per cent in 1984, 72 to 78 per cent in more developed regions, and 29 to 36 per cent in less developed regions.

This trend of an increasing proportion of young people living in urban areas will accelerate in the future. The urban youth population is projected to be 565 million in the year 2000, which implies an increase of 38 per cent from 410 million in 1984 at the average annual growth rate of 2.0 per cent. On the other hand, the rural youth population will decrease from 512 million in 1984 to 496 million in 2000 at the annual growth rate of -0.2 per cent. The excess of urban over rural growth will therefore increase from 1.3 percentage points in 1970-1984 to 2.2 percentage points in 1984-2000, resulting in an accelerated rise in the proportion of youth residing in urban areas. The proportion of urban youth increased by 4 percentage points from 40 per cent in 1970 to 44 per cent in 1984, and will increase by 9 percentage points to 53 per cent in 2000.

More developed regions and less developed regions contribute to this trend in different ways. The increase in the proportion of young urban residents is projected to slow down in more developed regions, where the majority of youth are already urban residents and a further increase of the proportion is relatively difficult. This slowdown in more developed regions will be overriden by an accelerated increase in less developed regions, where the proportion of youth living in urban areas rose from 29 per cent in 1970 to 36 per cent in 1984 and will rise steeply to 47 per cent in 2000.

Among the major regions of the world, the largest increases in the proportion of youth residing in urban areas are projected for Africa (35.9 per cent in 1984 to 47.3 per cent in 2000), East Asia (35.1 per cent in 1984 to 46.6 per cent in 2000) and South Asia (30.4 per cent in 1984 to 41.5 per cent in 2000). The increases in Africa and South Asia are mainly attributable to the high growth rates of urban youth population between 1984 and 2000 (4.9 per cent in Africa and 3.6 per cent in South Asia). On the other hand, a substantial decline in the growth rate of the urban youth population is projected in East Asia. However, the decline in the growth of the youth population in rural areas in East Asia will be even greater than in urban areas, resulting in a significant increase of the urban youth population relative to its rural counterpart.

Table 5. Annual growth rate of urban and rural youth population, world and regions, 1970-2000
(Percentage)

Youth population	1970-1984	1984-2000
World		
Urban	3.1	2.0
Rural	1.8	-0.2
More developed regions		
Urban	1.1	0.0
Rural	-1.3	-2.3
Less developed regions		
Urban	4.6	2.9
Rural	2.2	0.0

continued

Table 5 (continued)

Youth population	1970–1984	1984–2000
Africa		
Urban	5.4	4.9
Rural	2.2	1.9
Latin America		
Urban	4.0	2.3
Rural	0.8	−0.1
North America		
Urban	1.1	−3.0
Rural	−0.6	−2.2
East Asia		
Urban	3.5	0.8
Rural	1.8	−2.2
South Asia		
Urban	4.6	3.6
Rural	2.5	0.6
Europe		
Urban	1.2	−0.4
Rural	−1.2	−2.3
Oceania		
Urban	2.4	1.0
Rural	−0.2	−0.7
USSR		
Urban	1.4	0.7
Rural	−1.0	−2.3

Source: Department of International Economic and Social Affairs of the United Nations Secretariat.

Male and female youth population

Currently, the number of males aged 15-24 exceeds that of females. In 1984, there were 470 million males and 452 million females in this age group. The sex ratio, defined as the number of men per 100 women, is 103.9. This is somewhat greater than the sex ratio of 100.8 for the total global population. The higher sex ratio of the youth population reflects the tendency for the sex ratio of population to decline with age, which is a combined result of excess male over female births and higher female than male survival rates.

The ratio of male to female youth in the world has changed only slightly since 1950. It decreased from 104.3 in 1950 to 104.0 in 1960 and to 103.9 in 1984, and is projected to decline continuously to 103.7 in 1990, then rise again to 103.9 in 2000. The difference in the sex ratio between more developed regions (104.2) and less developed regions (103.8) is not significantly large.

The regional variation in the sex ratio, however, is not negligible. The excess of male over female youth population is most pronounced in Oceania (105.4), South Asia (105.1), Europe (104.9) and East Asia (104.2). The excess is of a lesser extent in the USSR (103.7) and North America (103.2), and substantially diminished in Latin America (101.6) and Africa (100.6). Different factors are responsible for these regional differentials. The lower level of mortality tends to be associated with the higher sex ratio at the young ages, because the sex differential in the number of births is kept more or less intact as the survival rate from birth to the age group approaches to one for both males and females. This is considered partly responsible for relatively high sex ratios of youth population in the regions that are entirely or predominantly more developed and low sex ratios in Africa and Latin America. On the other hand, the high youth sex ratio in South Asia is attributable to the unexpectedly small sex differentials in mortality that are widely observed in the region.

Youth in the age structure of population

The youth population comprised 19.4 per cent of the total world population in 1984, which means that one out of five inhabitants was a youth. Young people comprised 16.1 per cent of the total population in more developed regions, and 20.4 per cent in the less developed regions, reflecting the younger age structure of the less developed regions.

The proportion of the world youth population decreased from 18.5 per cent in 1950 to 16.9 per cent in 1965, then rose to 18.8 per cent in 1975. The proportion has since been growing slowly, reaching 19.4 per cent in 1984. The slow increase is projected to continue to 19.5 per cent in 1990, then fall to 17.3 per cent in 2000 and 16.0 per cent in 2025 (table 2). In sum, the trend of youth's share of population in the second half of the twentieth century is marked by a decrease in 1950-1965, an increase in 1965-1990, and a decrease in 1990-2000.

The proportion of the youth population changes when the 15-24 age group grows at a different rate from the rest of the population. An analysis of age-specific growth rates in different periods reveals that an important factor contributing to this fluctuating trend is the aging of the cohort born in the post-war decade. As they were born in rapidly increasing numbers, they raised the growth rate of children, then that of youth, and, as their aging proceeds, is currently raising the growth rate of the middle-aged. Because a higher growth rate of age groups other than youth tends to reduce the proportion of the population in the 15-24 group, the passage of the cohort through the young age range produced the down-up-down sequence in the proportion of youth population observed above. Another factor responsible for the trend is the previously mentioned fertility reduction in the 1970s, which contributed to the forecasted fall of youth's share of the population in the

1990s. The decline in the proportion of the youth population will continue
after 2000, when the age structure of the population becomes older as a result
of slower population growth.

The down-up-down sequence in the proportion of the youth population
during the second half of the century will be observed in many of the major
regions with somewhat different timing of trough and peak. In Latin America,
North America, South Asia, Europe, Oceania and the USSR the proportion of the
youth population reached a peak some time in the past ten years and will
decrease between now and the year 2000, although a small rise is projected in
the 1990s in the USSR. A somewhat "lagged" pattern will be seen in East Asia,
where the proportion of the youth population is still increasing at present,
and is projected to decrease very sharply after a peak around 1990. A notable
exception is Africa, where the proportion of the youth population in the year
2000 is forecasted to be larger than that in 1984.

III. GENERAL TRENDS IN THE FIRST HALF OF THE 1980s

In this chapter, an attempt is made to connect the demographic profile elaborated earlier with the specific issues to be detailed in subsequent chapters. The basic structural features of the global social and economic crisis are examined, as are the linkages between these features and the global situation of youth. This is an issue of prime importance. There is much evidence, now, to show that the recession in the international economic system, as it moves down the line of linkages to the grass roots of any society, has a progressively sharper impact on the poorest and most vulnerable sections of the population. It has been estimated, in this context, that a 1 per cent fall in the rate of growth of the developed countries appears to produce a 1.5 per cent fall in the average rate of growth of the developing countries. Within these countries, the impact mushrooms as it passes down to the poorest sections of the society. Thus, a 2 or 3 per cent decline in the average income of a developing country could plausibly result in a 10 to 15 per cent decline in the income of the poor within it. 1/ By means such as these, the major burdens of the world recession are often imposed upon those people who are least able to sustain them. In this chapter, the process is examined; in the next, it will be seen how more and more young people are increasingly incorporated into such vulnerable population groups.

In recent years, the world has witnessed two major recessions: in 1974-1975 and in 1980-1983. During the first recession, gross domestic product (GDP) growth in the developed market economies rose by 6.1 per cent in 1973, only 0.8 per cent in 1974, fell to 0.4 per cent in 1975, and climbed back up to 4.7 per cent in 1976. The situation of the developing countries was somewhat better. Their GDP growth was 7.4 per cent in 1973, dropped to 5.9 per cent in 1974 and 4 per cent in 1975, and then rose to 6.3 per cent in 1976. 2/

The second recession lasted much longer than the first, and was much sharper for the developing countries (table 6). In the developed market economies, GDP grew by 3.5 per cent in 1976-1980, and then dropped steadily to 1.6 per cent in 1981, and -0.3 per cent in 1982. 3/ In 1983, it began to rise again, to 2.4 per cent, and was estimated to have been 4.7 per cent in 1984. In the centrally planned economies, the net material product (NMP) growth rate was 4.6 per cent in 1976-1980, dropped to 2.4 per cent in 1981, and then began to rise slowly, to 3.7 per cent in 1982, 4.5 per cent in 1983, and was estimated to have remained at the same level, 4.5 per cent, in 1984. In the developing countries, however, the impact of the second recession was more severe. They had fared better in the first recession because it was shorter, and also because their heavy borrowing allowed them to continue growing. However, as a result of the second recession, the availability of foreign capital declined severely after 1981. This imposed considerable pressure on the developing countries, in particular on those which had come to rely upon foreign loans as a principal way of escaping the recession. The developing countries' GDP growth rates were thus 5.0 per cent in 1976-1980, dropped to 1.6 per cent in 1981, and further to 0.5 per cent in 1982 and 0.3 per cent in 1983, and were estimated to have risen to 2.9 per cent in 1984.

Table 6. Recent trends in world output
(Annual percentage change)

Country grouping	1976–1980	1981	1982	1983	1984 a/
Developed countries with market economies	3.5	1.6	−0.3	2.4	4.7
North America	3.6	2.7	−2.3	3.6	7.0
Europe	3.0	−0.3	0.5	1.2	2.3
Other	4.7	4.1	2.6	2.4	4.8
Developing countries (mainly market-oriented)	5.0	1.6	0.5	0.3	2.9
Africa	4.4	−1.0	0.5	−0.3	1.7
South and East Asia	6.0	6.6	3.5	5.5	5.3
West Asia	4.0	−1.1	−0.5	−0.2	4.0
Western Hemisphere	5.2	0.7	−1.4	−2.5	1.6
Other	4.7	2.6	2.5	0.8	2.4
Countries with centrally planned economies b/	4.6	2.4	3.7	4.5	4.5
China	6.0	4.8	7.4	8.5	7.0
Eastern Europe	3.9	−1.8	–	3.6	3.9
USSR	4.3	3.3	3.9	3.9	3.6

Source: 1985 Report on World Social Situation (United Nations publication, Sales No. E.85.IV.2).

a/ Preliminary figure.

b/ Net material product.

These figures indicate that from the beginning of 1983 there has been a limited improvement in the global economic situation, as a result of some reversal of recessionary trends. Recovery, however, has not become general. The negative consequences of the recession will be present for a considerable period of time. Evidence of economic recovery is different from various regions. Some parts of the world, such as North America, and some developing countries in South and East Asia, are in the midst of a rapid advance in income and output. In North America, however, the 7 per cent GDP growth rate estimated for 1984 must be balanced with the 1.3 per cent annual growth rate estimated for the first quarter of 1985. 4/ In the centrally planned economies, economic growth has accelerated, though its rate remains generally lower than in previous years. In China, the NMP growth rate was 6 per cent in 1976–1980, dropped to 4.8 per cent in 1981, then rose to 7.4 per cent in 1982 and 8.5 per cent in 1983, and dropped slightly to an estimated 7 per cent in 1984. In the USSR, comparable figures were 4.3 per cent (1976–1980), 3.3 per cent (1981), 3.9 per cent (1982 and 1983) and 3.6 per cent (1984 estimate). For Eastern Europe, a 3.9 per cent growth rate for 1976–1980, dropped to −1.8 per cent in 1981, then rose to 3.6 per cent in 1983, and was estimated to be 3.9 per cent

in 1984.   In the developed market economies of Western Europe, recovery has
thus far been limited.   GDP growth rates of 3 per cent in 1976-1980 dropped to
-0.3 per cent in 1981, and then rose slowly from 0.5 per cent in 1982, 1.2 per
cent in 1983, to an estimated 2.3 per cent in 1984.

In most developing countries, the recovery is even more qualified.   The
international environment was not favourable for them in the period after
1973, and became even less so after 1979-1980.   The slowing of growth in the
industrialized countries had negative effects, to a greater or lesser degree,
on most developing countries.   Those that were exporters of neither oil nor
manufactures suffered the most.   The effect on oil-exporting countries came
more slowly, since it was initially offset by the rise in petroleum prices.
The generally high levels of inflation in the late 1970s helped most debtor
countries.   However, the sharp rise in interest rates after 1979 hurt many of
them, particularly in Latin America.   In general terms, the economic
instability of the 1970s - of prices, exchange rates and interest rates -
complicated the tasks of the developing countries.   There is at present no
concrete evidence that these complications have been entirely removed.   GDP
growth rates for the developing countries have been cited above.   These
averages, however, conceal much regional variation.   At the two extremes are
South and East Asia (excluding China), with growth rates of 6 per cent
(1976-1980), 6.6 per cent (1981), 3.5 per cent (1982), 5.5 per cent (1983) and
5.3 per cent (1984 estimate) which did not suffer so badly, and Africa, with
rates of 4.4 per cent (1976-1980), -1 per cent (1981), 0.5 per cent (1982),
-0.3 per cent (1983), and 1.7 per cent (1984 estimate), which was hit
extremely hard.   For the developing countries, then, as a group, the outlook
continues to be bleak: they are confronted with problems which seriously
hamstring their prospects for a vigorous reactivation of development.

This examination of world output statistics should be conflated with
figures of world trade.   Here the situation is worse, and reflects the uneven
character of world economic recovery.   For the first time in decades, an
increase in world output was not accompanied by a proportionate increase in
world imports - which remained virtually stagnant during 1983-1984.   Strong
rates of import growth were registered only in North America, a few developing
countries in Asia, and some centrally planned economies, notably China and the
USSR.   However, real imports fell in Japan and remained stagnant in Western
Europe.   Even worse was a sharp decline in import volumes in most developing
countries.   In the last few years, a large number of countries, from different
groupings, have adjusted to external imbalances by cutting the imports which
would have been others' exports.   This has tended to increase surplus world
export capacity and unemployment, while domestic needs in many parts of the
world remain unsatisfied.

Not merely in international trade, but in the international financial
system as well, the cumulative effects of recent events could continue to be
baneful.   Protectionist measures have multiplied, and the transfer of capital
to developing countries has greatly diminished.   The recent surge of imports
into North America, as it recovered from recession, was partly financed by an
inflow of capital from other countries.   Some of these were developing
countries, which can ill afford such measures.   Persistently high interest
rates have contributed to the funnelling of savings from essentially capital-
short to capital-surplus countries.   By 1983, capital-short developing
countries were close to becoming net exporters of capital to other countries.
It appears evident, then, that a reactivation of development can only take
place if the international financial and trading system is reinvigorated, and
the economic recovery - so far tenuous - is strengthened.

However, because of a number of uncertainties in the policy stances of major actors in the world economy, and considerable unevenness in the recovery, the outlook for the future is not entirely clear. There is considerable divergence in the policy stances in different regions, and this does not always conduce to a shared and concurrent global improvement. Among the developed market economies, the upswing in North America, continued growth in Japan, and limited recovery in Western Europe are qualified by differences over the issues of fiscal and monetary policy, structural budget deficits, and high interest rates. Among the centrally planned economies, strong performance in the Asian countries, continued growth in the USSR, and limited recovery in the Eastern European countries are qualified by the fact that some countries borrowed substantially in the 1970s and faced increased debt service payments and a drying up of credit in recent years. Further, there has been evidence of a reduced level of commercial and financial exchanges between the developed market economies and the centrally planned economies. This appears to be a reflection not merely of recession and the international debt situation, but also of problems that were extra-economic in origin and generally detrimental to international co-operation.

With the exception of some countries in South and East Asia, the situation for most developing countries is very difficult. Many of them are emerging from the recession with a legacy of difficulties that is not likely to be dissipated by recovery elsewhere. While the impact of recession takes time to work through the channels which lead down to the poorest sections of any society, this is equally, or perhaps more, the case with the impact of economic recovery. The legacy of difficulties is particularly acute in two contexts: famine and debt-service burdens. The tragedy of famine, despite abundant food supplies in global markets, is eloquent testimony of major imbalances in the international system. One consequence of recession was a deep depression in commodity markets. This sharply cut the purchasing power of many countries in sub-Saharan Africa. The consequence, combined with a drought that began in 1982, was severe hunger and malnutrition for 150 million people. While relief operations have been considerable, the crisis is by no means over: 21 countries in sub-Saharan Africa continue to be threatened by famine, 6 of them particularly severely. 5/

The external debt has reached a critical level in some developing countries, and is a serious problem in several others. Many countries are now in a very precarious balance-of-payments position. Debt-service ratios, particularly in Latin America, are likely to remain extremely high, even after recovery in the developed countries. Debtor countries will still be compelled to continue drastic retrenchment, and most developing countries have had to take very sharp adjustment measures. A general consequence is the lack of new finance, which hinders new development efforts, as well as the sustenance of existing ones. The situation is unlikely to show any drastic improvement through the rest of this decade. A recent projection indicates that by 1990 most developing countries will still be using more of their exports to finance external debt than they did in 1980. 6/

The social implications of these global economic tendencies have been extremely baneful in many parts of the world. This is particularly so in developing countries, most of which have no reserve "safety net" to dampen the effects of economic hardship and austerity. The social cost of economic adjustments for recession has been very high, and even onerous in certain areas. These adjustments have had a general contractionary effect, and the biggest squeeze has been on social development investments. Most countries are fast approaching the limits of contractionary adjustment; import levels cannot be further reduced without dangerous consequences - economic, social

and even political. In almost one out of every four developing countries,
per capita output has fallen in the last few years. Fiscal austerity has led
to curtailed assistance for lower-income groups, and open unemployment has
reached unusually high levels. The result has been much hardship for
economically weaker sections of the population: and herein lies the
significance of these global economic trends for the situation of youth,
particularly since a majority of young people live in the less developed
regions of the world.

One way of assessing the impact of recession upon youth is to examine
some of the major channels through which it is transmitted. Family income is
one such channel. In many parts of the world, the result of recession and
general inflation has been a sharp fall in average real income. In the Latin
American region, for example, average incomes have now been in decline for
several consecutive years. In Brazil, income per person fell by over 4 per
cent in 1981 and by almost another 2 per cent in 1982. In Chile, per capita
GNP fell by 15 per cent in a single year (1981), and in Costa Rica real incomes
have fallen by as much as one third. 7/ Statistics taken over a longer span
of time do not paint a substantially brighter picture. Thus, for the period
1960-1982, average annual growth rates of per capita GNP were 0.6 per cent in
Haiti, 1 per cent in Honduras, 1 per cent in El Salvador, 0.2 per cent in
Nicaragua, 1 per cent in Peru, 0.7 per cent in Ecuador, and 0.6 per cent in
Chile. 8/

In Africa, the impact has been the most severe. In more than half the
countries of the region, real per capita income is in fact less than it was a
decade ago. The cumulative impact of recession, inflation, drought and war
resulted in an estimated 2 per cent fall in sub-Saharan Africa's GNP per capita
between 1979 and 1980. 9/ Such averages are useful general indicators, but
they often disguise even steeper declines among poor and unemployed sections
of the population. Even over a longer time-span, from 1960 to 1982, several
African countries showed falling per capita GNP annual growth rates: Chad
(-2.8 per cent), Zaire (-0.3 per cent), Uganda (-1.1 per cent), Somalia
(-0.1 per cent), Niger (-1.5 per cent), Madagascar (-0.5 per cent), Ghana
(-1.3 per cent), Sudan (-0.4 per cent), and Zambia (-0.1 per cent). 10/ Many
of these countries are dependent upon raw material exports to the developed
countries. Through the recession, commodity markets for such raw materials
were peculiarly depressed, and continue to be so. In 1982, for instance,
world prices of copper fell to their lowest level in 50 years. In Zambia,
which is a major exporter of copper, Government capital expenditure has been
cut by two-thirds, and average incomes have nearly been halved in recent
years. 11/

Another major channel through which recession is transmitted to the lives
of young people is cut-backs in Government services for children and youth.
Social welfare programmes for youth frequently suffer rapidly and disproportionately from any forced cut-backs in Government expenditure. This
happens in both developed and developing countries. It is difficult to
generalize, in global terms, about causes of the phenomenon. In a large
number of cases, however, there does appear to be a common denominator: the
belief that social welfare programmes for children and youth are "uneconomic".
Considerable evidence can be adduced to establish that this belief is of
questionable validity. Yet this does not indicate desuetude of the belief,
nor detract from its apparent popularity. Another apparent reason for cuts in
social welfare programmes for the young is that they are seldom protected by
powerful interest groups. While several other reasons could be found, the end
result is usually the same. Under the impact of recession, the share of
Government expenditure devoted to basic needs programmes has declined in many
parts of the world. Thus, one set of estimates of housing, community, social

security and welfare expenditures, between 1972 and 1981, as a percentage of total central Governments expenditure, show decline, stagnation, or at best, marginal increases. In the low-income economies, the figures for 1972 and 1981 showed a slight increase, from 4.7 to 5 per cent. The middle-income economies showed a sharp decline, from 20.3 to 13.8 per cent. The high-income oil-exporting economies also registered a decline, from 12.5 to 9.5 per cent. Finally, in the developed market economies, there was a small increase, from 36.4 to 41.7 per cent. 12/ Here again, the impact has clearly been the most severe on the developing countries in general.

The International Development Strategy for the Third United Nations Development Decade postulates a harmonious international environment which would encourage and support national and collective developmental efforts. But such an environment has been conspicuously absent in the first few years of the Decade. 13/ The instability in the world economy has been exacerbated by strained international co-operation and continued political and military conflict. As noted earlier, an average of 37,000 people have died every month since the end of the Second World War, as a result of about 150 different armed conflicts in various parts of the world. In 1983 alone, 40 separate armed conflicts were identified, involving 75 countries and about 4 million soldiers. These 40 conflicts together claimed at least 1 million lives. 14/

Conflicts such as these have a whole gamut of negative consequences which often appear in insidious ways. Thousands of people lose their homes, sometimes even their countries, and are driven into penury and destitution. Large influxes of refugees mean not only suffering for the refugees themselves, but also major economic and social stress for the recipient countries, which are often poor and stretched to their limits in any case. The immediate consequences of military conflicts, such as direct damage to the productive capacity or the economic infrastructure, are underscored by less tangible and possibly longer-lasting effects: discredited authority, bitter social divisions, debased institutions, and generally brutalized populations. The aftermath of particular concern in this context is the debilitation, disillusionment, and even decimation of the young. The Second World War provides a paradigm of what major conflicts can do to the youth population in major areas of conflict.

Military expenditure, upon the global level, has reached formidable proportions. While there are many difficulties in standardizing statistics here, 15/ some estimates are available as general indicators. As a share of the world gross national product (GNP), total military spending declined between the early 1950s and the late 1970s, after which it started to increase. Since 1980, the growth of military expenditure has consistently outpaced increases in global output. An estimate of global military spending in 1984 arrives at a figure of over $900 billion. 16/ This represents a startling average of $130 for each person in the world, and is equivalent to more than the average income of several developing countries. By way of specific example, it has been estimated that the cost of a single new nuclear submarine is equal to the annual education budget of 23 developing countries with a total of 160 million school-going children. 17/ All this provides some illustration of what could be achieved, on the global scale, if even half the resources devoted to the military were invested in social development. The relationship between disarmament and development is, of course, an extremely complex one. However, military spending and social programmes are often in competition with each other, not merely in terms of resources, but also in the crucial area of attitudes and perceptions. 18/ The impact of escalating military spending on young people, then, seems to have been doubly negative: resources lost to social development activities, and plaudits accruing to the attitudes and perceptions of militarism.

Another prerequisite for achieving the goals of the International Development Strategy is the full and effective participation of the entire population in development, including vulnerable groups such as women, children, disabled persons and youth. 19/ Yet, progress in securing this effective participation has been very limited. While there has been some evidence of involvement in the process of social change, as well as in the articulation of specific interests on the part of these groups, this is not a general configuration. 20/ In some parts of the developing world, such as East and South Asia, the standards of living of large numbers of people have improved. Elsewhere, however, particularly in Africa, poverty has increased considerably. In many countries of Latin America, both poor and middle-income social groups have experienced a deterioration in their living conditions. Disparities in income have continued to be very large, the goal of full employment ever more difficult to reach.

In a bleak milieu such as this, the situation of young people the world over continues to be very tenuous. The picture becomes even less bright when global economic and social trends are considered in the light of the demographic profile of youth detailed above. Even though it is not possible to see youth as a monolithic social group, with identical experiences and responses, there is little doubt, as will be argued below, that young people often constitute the most vulnerable sections of different social groups and classes. This proviso notwithstanding, young people still constitute a generational group which, in spite of the heterogeneity of its components and their specific experience, still undergoes a socializing process within concrete historical and structural conditions. There are thus certain common features which enable youth to play a specific social role, though this may assume different forms in different kinds of societies. Consequently, it becomes possible to perceive youth as a relatively autonomous social group which has its own characteristic social aspirations and behaviour.

It follows then that the problems affecting young people have a certain universal dimension, but take on a specific character according to the ways in which they are seen or felt. In the 1980s, the major problem areas that affect young people, across the global spectrum, are those concerning development, the family, the world of work, and culture. In general terms, the integration of young people in the development process has clearly been insufficient. The problems of unemployment and underemployment worsen implacably. The relationship of young people with their families becomes increasingly fragile as a result of a variety of exogenous pressures. Much cultural ferment has been in evidence. The process of socialization of youth is no longer a simple transmission, through the family, of accepted values, attitudes and roles. Economic recession has not stopped social change; in some cases it has intensified it. Thus, in many parts of the world, traditional systems of authority and values are being steadily supplanted by ideas and attitudes which do not yet constitute a coherent frame of reference. At the same time, these new ideas create expectations which are impossible to satisfy in a period of contracting social policy. In all these variegated processes of change, young people play a double, apparently contradictory role: on the one hand, they are active agents of the process of social change; on the other hand, they often suffer as a result of it.

During periods of social and economic crisis, the negative part of this dichotomy is generally more prominent: the young suffer more because they are demonstrably more vulnerable. The other, more positive, option is, of course, available: that the crisis itself could be overcome, to a certain degree, by using youth as an active agency for social change, and thus capitalizing on its vast potential for generating development. That young people constitute a major resource for the development process is unquestionable. However, there has been little unanimity on how exactly this resource should be utilized. As pointed out in chapter I, various solutions have been adopted. These solutions display marked regional, national and even local diversities. Moreover, there is a general tendency towards fragmentation in the identification of the specific problems of youth, as well as in implementing policies to ameliorate these problems.

This fragmentation is engendered by the fact that the social component of development has been neglected in favour of a narrow economic conception. 21/ Positive policies for social welfare, as noted above, have often been rejected on the grounds of being "uneconomic". Economic development, it has been believed, would, ipso facto, generate social development. In many cases, it has not in fact done so. There are several examples of developing countries where rapid economic growth has done little to resolve major social disequilibria. It is becoming increasingly evident that accelerated economic growth can in fact co-exist with the reproduction of social inequalities and the maintenance of wide sectors of the population in a state of destitution. 22/ Many young people are destitute, and, as the next chapter attempts to show, many more continue to become marginalized. From the point of view of youth, therefore, there is considerable need for positive social development policies.

Unfortunately, there are often serious deficiencies in social policies. These tend to be fragmented sectorally, and have a high degree of dispersion. Thus, the mechanisms of society concerned with planning for youth often occupy a peripheral position in the political and administrative structure. Although, in recent years, the relationship between economic planning and social planning has tended to become less biased in favour of the former, fragmentation has often remained an attribute of the latter. Thus has social planning proceeded upon the traditional assumptions that the social space can be comprehended within the categories of the so-called "social sectors": education, employment, health etc. This has tended to denature the essentially human concerns of development, as well as fragment, rather than integrate, these different social sectors. In the context of many national youth policies, the result is often a weak linkage between general aims and principles on the one hand, and specific programmes of action on the other. The problem is exacerbated by a dispersion in the process of implementation: a variety of governmental and non-governmental agencies are responsible for different components of the youth policy, and there is insufficient integration of these various efforts. Moreover, while the differentiation of responsibility between the various agencies should be based upon dynamic criteria of social needs, it often ends up being based upon criteria of mere administrative convenience. Consequently, many vital needs of different sub-groups of young people, in many different areas, are neglected.

Dispersion and fragmentation also frequently characterize the linkages between the national, regional and international levels of youth policy and planning. There is therefore a great need to streamline the flow of ideas and operational initiatives, upward from the national level, and downward from the international level, with regional bridges linking the two. Thus, in the present chapter, an attempt has been made to conflate specific demographic data with general social and economic trends, and so arrive at a composite picture of the situation of youth. In the following chapters, the focus is sharpened in order to examine the particular issues that inform this general situation.

Notes

1/ United Nations Children's Fund, The State of the World's Children, 1984 (New York, Oxford University Press, 1984), pp. 69-70.

2/ World Bank, World Development Report 1984 (New York, Oxford University Press, 1984), p. 11.

3/ All macro-economic data for this section, unless otherwise indicated, are drawn from World Economic Survey 1984: Current Trends and Policies in the World Economy (United Nations publication, Sales No. E.84.II.C.1) and 1985 Report on the World Social Situation (United Nations publication, Sales No. E.85.IV.2).

4/ Figures from United States Commerce Department, reported in the The Guardian Weekly, 132, No. 17 (28 April 1985), p. 7.

5/ For a general discussion on the food crisis in Africa, see "The food crisis in Africa in the context of global production and trade", annex to World Economic Survey 1984, ..., annex, pp. 98-104.

6/ International Monetary Fund, World Economic Outlook, April 1985 (Washington, D.C., 1985).

7/ The State of the World's Children, 1984 ..., pp. 69-70.

8/ World Bank, op. cit., pp. 218-219, table 1.

9/ The State of the World's Children, 1984 ...., pp. 69-70.

10/ World Bank, op. cit.

11/ The State of the World's Children, 1984 ....

12/ World Bank, op. cit., pp. 268-269, table 26.

13/ "Review and appraisal of the International Development Strategy for the Third United Nations Development Decade: Report of the Secretary-General" (A/39/115 - E/1984/49, 29 March 1984).

14/ 1985 Report on the World Social Situation ..., pp. 14-23.

15/ "Report of the Secretary-General on general and complete disarmament" (A/39/348, 31 August 1984).

16/ Ibid., p. 22, and Stockholm International Peace Research Institute, SIPRI Yearbook, 1984 (London, 1984), p. 64.

17/ 1985 Report on the World Social Situation ..., pp. 14-23.

18/ Report of the Secretary-General on the Relationship between Disarmament and Development (United Nations publication, Sales No. E.82.IX.1).

19/ International Development Strategy of the Third United Nations Development Decade (United Nations publication, 1981), p. 7.

20/ "Report of the Secretary-General on social aspects of development" (A/39/171-E/1984/54, 24 April 1984).

21/   See P. Streeten, <u>The Frontiers of Development Studies</u> (London, Macmillan, 1972), pp. 13-20.

22/   See P. Streeten and F. Stewart, <u>New Strategies for Development: Poverty, Income Distribution and Growth</u>, Oxford Economic Papers, vol. 28, 1976; M. S. Ahluwalia, "Inequality, poverty and development", <u>Journal of Development Economics</u>, No. 3, 1976, pp. 307-342; and Michael Lipton, <u>Why Poor People Stay Poor: A Study of Urban Bias in the World</u> (London, Temple Smith, 1977).

IV. GENERAL PROBLEMS IN THE FIRST HALF OF THE 1980s

It would appear to have been established, thus far, that young people constitute a group that is particularly vulnerable to the effects of the global crisis. Conversely, the way out of the crisis – the development process – is also closely linked to the situation of youth and their possible participation in it. Herein lies the essential dynamic of the situation of young people: they are often agents of social change; but equally often, they are the victims of that very change. The early 1980s have been a period of considerable economic and social transformation in the world at large. The involvement of young people in this process has been of the dual nature elaborated above. It follows then, that the crucial need during the rest of the decade, from the point of view of youth, is to minimize their marginaliza- tion and to maximize their participation in the development process. An important element in planning for this would be an assessment of how the situation of young people has changed and developed globally, and in the major regions of the world, in recent years. This chapter, therefore, attempts such an assessment, dealing with the general problems as they appear at the mid-point of the decade. It follows the consideration of general trends in the previous chapter, and leads to an examination, in the next chapter, of the regional manifestations of these general trends and problems.

For all the regional diversity, there is still a global nexus that could be established vis-à-vis the situation of youth. Some problems are universal, even though they may manifest themselves in ways that are unique to each region. The problems that young people face, after all, are not ends unto themselves. They are merely reflections of the larger problems of society in general. So should they be analysed within the larger framework of global and regional social and economic structures, with, of course, a specific emphasis upon the social, economic and cultural elements that together constitute the general category of youth.

Marginalization

Before moving on to an assessment of the major issues confronting young people in the 1980s, it is important to look carefully at the manner in which different kinds of youth are integrated into different levels in society. Of crucial significance here is the position of young people who are in so-called marginal situations. They happen to be particularly vulnerable to the social stresses and pressures that are an inevitable concomitant of the development process. Despite many efforts and initiatives, the process of their marginalization continues inexorably. It is thus a vital necessity for development planning to proceed upon assumptions that are informed by the special needs and problems of these sub-groups.

The concept of marginality is a wide one, encompassing a variety of situations and cases. 1/ It is not merely a problem of economic under- development, but social underdevelopment as well. It is therefore a multidimensional concept, and must be seen as such. Young people who are "marginal" may therefore be poor, incompletely urbanized, culturally unassimilated, spatially segregated, and often peripheral to much of society. Yet they are a part of it; often a large one. Marginality is consequently a plural and relative condition. Economically, it implies a situation of being on the periphery of the major economic structures of society. Politically, it means no participation in party, electoral, local or other modes of decision- making. Psychological marginality is caused by a lack of personality attributes appropriate to life in modern society, from work habits and consumption- orientation to scientific ways of thought and rational conceptions of self and society. Cultural marginality means being cut off from the mainstream, by differences, for example, of language or life-style. If the concept of culture is seen in its widest sense, then marginality happens when people come to accept the values of the dominant culture, but lack the means to achieve them, or are prevented from doing so by various kinds of social constraints.

Marginality is often caused by situations of cultural transition which result in inadequate adjustment: migration, educational mobility, marriage, or external influences across boundaries of any kind of social group - one locality to another, one country to another, one occupation to another, even one generation to another. Youth, by its very social nature, has to make such cultural transitions frequently, and becomes marginalized as a result.

Young people in marginal situations are thus in a position which is as difficult to categorize as it is to ameliorate. They are not socially functional, because they often derive less from the society and economy than they contribute to it. Neither are they in a dysfunctional position, because the societies in which they are could well integrate and support them. They are not even afunctional, because their role, while it may be insufficiently appreciated, is still significant to the functioning of the social system in one way or another.

There are many sub-groups of youth that happen to be in marginal situations. Perhaps the biggest one is young women: women are marginalized in general, young women in particular. This is not to say that all women are in marginal situations, but only to draw attention to the fact that many of them are. While their marginality is a multidimensional phenomenon, there is one specific area that is perhaps the most crucial. Often omitted from all official statistics, housewives make a huge contribution to both economy and society through under-valued, unappreciated and unpaid domestic labour. Women's household labour, if given economic value, would add an estimated one third, or $4,000,000,000,000 to the world's GNP. 2/ This does not apply merely to housewives. In many developing countries, young female children seldom have the luxury of being "young" at all. They are integrated into the labour force before they enter their teens, often as domestic and family labour. Rural women account for more than half the food produced in the developing countries. They account for as much as 80 per cent of the food produced in Africa. 2/ By the time many young girls reach the age of youth, they often have two jobs, one of which - household labour - they are not paid for. When they do work, for instance in the manufacturing industry, they earn, on a global average, 25 per cent less than men in the same jobs. 2/ Women in some parts of the service sector of the economy are even worse off. The personal service sector, for instance, is a huge one, particularly in the cities of less developed regions. In a major city of Latin America, 60 per cent of working women are maids. There are 200,000 of them. Some 72 per cent live in with the families that employ them, on call 24 hours a day, with one or two days off in a month, and no normal social life. Three quarters of them are from rural areas, and illiterate. Four out of five get less than the official minimum wage and are less than 20 years of age. Some 60,000 are between 8 and 14 years old. 3/ Patterns of this kind are replicated in many parts of the world.

Many other young people live on the margins of society: young migrants and refugees, who face a situation of inadequate cultural and educational transmission in an alien environment; young workers, who struggle on the margins of the labour force, hired or fired as needed, and meagrely paid when they do work; disabled young people, who face a perpetual social stigma as they attempt to participate more fully in the society that spawns and then rejects them; young people who are often driven by social circumstances into an increasingly articulated machinery of crime and deviance. In many situations, students are also a marginalized sub-group. Though they may be integrated into the formal educational structure, they are often victims of the disjunction between education and the world of work, as well as of an increasingly inadequate socialization process.

There are many more young people in positions and situations that are difficult to categorize, but their predicaments are real, and very often tragic. As workers, they are poorly paid for long hours of work, often in impermanent, hard-labour, dirty and dangerous occupations which do not make them eligible for even the meagre social security benefits that do exist. They often live in environments that make a mockery of the term "housing": shanty towns, old slums, new tenements, and sometimes simply on pavements. As consumers, they lack the purchasing power to acquire the goods and services that are enjoyed by the rest of society. Socially, their status brings them only insult and injury. Culturally, they are outsiders; most lack formal education and sometimes even the ability to speak the national language.

All these various kinds of young people, then, live on the periphery of society, struggling to join the mainstream, and often failing to do so. The category of marginality, as pointed out above, is necessarily a wide-ranging one, subsuming, as it does, such a complex variety of situations and cases. It is also a category with a wide overlap, since it could cover sections of the population that are normally included in other categories or sub-categories. Consideration of phenomena like unemployment establishes the point. In the United States, for instance, youth unemployment has been generally high, but it has been especially high among young Blacks. It was 75 per cent higher than unemployment among young Whites in the early 1960s and 150 per cent higher in the early 1980s. The general rate of unemployment among Blacks, who accounted for 11 per cent of the labour force in 1980, is nearly twice that of Whites. The rate of youth unemployment and general unemployment among the population of Hispanic origin is 50 per cent higher than the rate for Whites. In 1980, nearly two fifths of Black youth were out of work, as compared to one quarter of White youth. 4/ Another example may be taken from the case of Sweden, where unemployment among children of foreign workers is much higher than among Swedish youth. In the second quarter of 1979, unemployment rates for adolescents were 12.1 and 7.5 per cent, and for young adults 6.4 and 3.1 per cent, respectively. 4/ In cases such as these, one may thus speak of an overlap between unemployment and marginality.

Through the course of their lives, many people pass in and out of the fold of marginality, though it appears that more pass in than out. Concrete data to establish a global increase in marginality are not readily available, but a variety of general indicators seem to point in this direction, particularly vis-à-vis youth becoming marginalized. In the discussion that follows in the rest of this chapter, an attempt is made to adduce the relevant data.

Participation

Like the problem of marginality, another general problem is the participation of young people in development. The three forms of participation - political, economic and social - often overlap and are frequently interdependent. 5/ Political participation, a crucial element in the structure of society, is very controversial because it concerns the distribution of power. This makes it difficult to quantify and analyse.

Moreover, the frontiers between political participation and political mobilization have tended to become increasingly blurred. In any case, young people, particularly students, have often been deeply involved in this form of participation and have frequently articulated demands for a more democratic process of political participation. Economic participation, which implies the direct involvement of people in the management of their work, and in a sharing of its benefits, is easier to analyse. The position of young people here, though it has certainly improved over the years, is still tenuous. They constitute the younger and often impermanent section of the labour force which is not consulted in many workers' activities. Traditional structures of authority, often based upon a generational conception, tend to circumscribe the efforts of young people in this direction.

The position of marginalized groups of young people is particularly bad with regard to this form of participation. Social participation, which covers a great variety of activities, is seen here as the area of the involvement of young people in their immediate neighbourhood or community. As the socialization process within the traditional family becomes increasingly inadequate for a lot of young people, they tend to move out of its ambit into different forms of social association: peer groups within the educational structure, for instance. Several of these initiatives lack a definite direction, which is a reflection of the cultural crisis that many young people face in the 1980s. Common to all these forms of participation, then, appears to be the need to help young people in articulating their own specific interests, and to direct these initiatives into national youth policies and development plans.

A related issue is the participation of youth in various kinds of social movements, pursuing what has been described above as its transformative role. Global diversity notwithstanding, one general phenomenon appears to be the fact that schools, political parties, trade unions and even Governments appear to have entered the 1980s under the threat of a considerable withdrawal of confidence by young people at large. 6/ This is a defining characteristic of recession and hard times. Most people are preoccupied with the pragmatic, everyday struggle simply to survive, and social groups tend to close their ranks. If this situation continues, and spans the decade, it may become explosive, because many young people, barring perhaps the most affluent, may well begin to perceive the very fact of being young as a serious misfortune in the 1980s. They will be forced into this perception in the teeth of a radical lessening of expectations and a decline in the quality of life. When their aspirations for access to jobs, careers and self-respect are thwarted, it is not unlikely that their frustrations will find expression in powerful movements for defence of the economic and social rights of adulthood.

On the other hand, there appears to be some evidence to indicate that the 1980s may not be an era of youth movements as such. 7/ The early years of the decade have seen the involution of youth in many movements transcending earlier themes focussed upon the "generation gap": the ecology movement, the women's movement, the disarmament movement. Movements such as these, by their very nature, encompass many other age groups and elements of the population. Young people are thus not exclusively involved, although they might play a pivotal role in the movements. The role happens to be crucial because it is youth, after all, that will suffer the most in the event of a further deterioration in living and environmental conditions. The recognition of this, among ever-increasing numbers of young people, brings them to the centre of the stage in these movements. New influences, such as knowledge about, and experience of, the limitation of energy and ecological resources or other contemporary factors, will affect society as a whole in an extremely

significant way. An assessment of the situation of young people, and their
socialization, thus needs to be looked at, more than ever before, in the
context of what is generally called contemporary history. 8/

The various forms of participation, of course, evolve differently in
different types of societies. The assessment made above is particularly
apposite for the developed market economy countries. The activists of
participating movements in the 1960s and early 1970s were often university
students, and their causes were usually idealistic and directed at the purpose
and function of society. Apart from occasional movements, including some
anarchistic and underground ones, such political activism is less prevalent
now, and has been replaced by the broader movements described above. There
appears to have been a commensurate shift in tactics, from pitched battles in
the streets and on university campuses to less confrontational and more
coalesced activism, using political and legal channels to achieve well
specified objectives. On the part of Governments, there appears to be more
sensitivity to the pluralism of values and concerns which these participatory
movements reflect; more understanding of the social implications of certain
decisions; and less tendency to adopt purely sectoral approaches to problems. 9/

However, while the participatory processes have evolved a great deal,
there have been concomitant difficulties: local Government agencies have
encountered an increasingly heavy and complex workload; projects have been
delayed, often at great expense, because of various kinds of protests; special
interest groups have sometimes wielded disproportionate influence in getting
planning decisions in their favour; many groups - minorities and second-
generation immigrants for instance - have not been able to organize effectively
for the participatory process because of entrenched forms of discrimination.
Young people, as has been argued above, bear many of these burdens, often to a
disproportionate extent.

In the centrally planned economies, economic and social participation
through full employment, and political participation through the mobilization
of the populace for the achievement of collective goals, are essential
elements in the structure of society. Participatory forces tend to be
controlled by Governments, in order to organize them for the implementation of
national policy. Attempts have been made to decentralize these controls, and
participation is encouraged at the local level for solving local problems
within the context of collective goals. 9/ Among various participatory
groups, youth groups and leagues have played a significant role, particularly
in educational and cultural activities. In the area of economic participation,
the right to work is being increasingly supplemented by decentralized workers'
management initiatives. With regard to the position of young people vis-à-vis
economic participation, the major issues are discussed in the section on
employment, below.

In the developing countries, the struggle against poverty and the
building of a viable economy - often waged against the backdrop of another
struggle for national unity and cohesion - makes participation a necessity,
but one that is particularly difficult to achieve. For people whose only
concern is survival, and much of the population of developing countries lives
below the poverty line, participation - unless it means immediate and tangible
benefits - is just one more abstraction. In fact, the lower people are in the
social hierarchy, the less are they likely to participate in activities of
already existing organized groups. 10/ They rely, instead, upon alternative
forms of social association, and young people play a particularly active
role here. There is much evidence of this from among the urban poor and

marginalized groups in some developing countries. 11/ A major problem for the State has been to come to terms with such groups, establish channels of communication with them, monitor their self-help activities, and thus involve them in the participatory process. Governmental agencies have often encountered difficulties in dealing with this kind of community participation which are frequently a result of bureaucratic orthodoxies maintaining that participation takes too long to organize, costs too much in administrative overheads, and frequently requires unfamiliar changes in operational styles and procedures.

Many developing countries have seen other modes of participation that are engendered by economic grievance, cultural deprivation or political exclusion. A whole variety of movements can be considered here: spontaneous mass demonstrations against unpopular measures such as food price increases; large-scale squatting on privately owned lands in rural and urban areas; and subnational groups, defined along ethnic, linguistic or religious lines, seeking better terms of participation in society. In many cases, students have spearheaded such movements; in many other cases, young people have been actively involved in both leadership as well as rank and file. Several of these movements have achieved their objectives. But, in general terms, the developing countries still have many constraints upon the participation of youth in all levels of society. These, to mention some of them, include real and functional illiteracy, inadequate diffusion of information and poor communication networks outside the major cities; communities that are internally differentiated on the basis of, inter alia, age structure and status; deficiencies in systems of political representation that make Governments less responsive and accountable than they might otherwise be; and, finally, deficiencies in national youth policies.

Education

Problems related to the sector of education also have many common denominators that span the regions of the world. Especially since the 1960s, a critique of educational systems has been evolving, in both more and less developed regions. This has hinged essentially upon the unsuitability of educational systems to modern social needs, or, in more specific terms, the wide gap between formal schooling and the world of work. While considerable progress has been achieved, it is evident that educational reform has not kept pace with the rapid growth of the critique. In this context, the second half of the 1980s may well be crucial, because the apparatus of education is a manifestly vulnerable sector of society during periods of economic crisis. Young people the world over have participated, in various ways, in the development of critiques of education, and have articulated coherent demands for a further democratization of the educational process. While there has been evidence of much democratic transformation in terms of volume and quantity, this has not always been accompanied by a corresponding transformation of quality in the ways in which knowledge is transmitted.

Across the world, educational systems have recently encountered progressively increasing difficulties. Various trends, many of them characteristic of difficult times, have contributed to this: unfavourable economic conditions, recession, and the consequent financial squeeze, particularly on social development investments; demographic development seriously affecting school-entering cohorts of the population; changing attitudes and increasing skepticism towards education. Of all organized social activities, education is the one that directly involves the greatest number of people. It is visible, influential, complex, and, given the rapidly changing social milieu, full of uncertainties. 12/ It is not unlikely, therefore, that the whole issue of education should be one that is frequently a subject of public debate, conducted not merely by young people, but by society at large.

Public expenditure devoted to education for the world total, at current market prices, grew from $51.5 billion in 1960 to $627.6 billion in 1981 (table 7). 13/ These figures represented 3.6 per cent of the world GNP in 1960 and 5.7 per cent in 1981. The percentage was considerably lower for the developing countries, increasing from 2.3 per cent in 1960 to 4.1 per cent in 1981. For the developed countries, the percentage was 3.9 per cent in 1960, and it rose to 6.1 per cent in 1981. Computations of average expenditure on education per student make substantially the same point (table 8). 14/ The developed countries spent $2,272 per student (all levels of education) in 1981, which was 8.6 times more than the $264 they had spent in 1960. For the developing countries, the expenditure rose 6.9 times, from $32 per student in 1960 to $221 in 1981. The expenditure on each student in the developing countries was therefore less than 10 per cent of the expenditure on each student in the developed countries.

Enrolment trends, for all levels of education, including the pre-primary stage, have shown steady increases through the last two decades. 15/ These increases can be attributed, in the main, to efforts in the developing countries, since the decreasing school-age population in the developed countries has resulted in commensurate decreases in total numbers of pupils enrolled. Worldwide enrolment figures for regular education in the period from 1960 to 1982 have shown an increase from 455 million to 930 million. Enrolment in developing countries accounted for 57 per cent of the 1960 world total, and 70 per cent of the 1982 world total. It registered net absolute increases of 140 million between 1960 and 1970, and 266 million between 1970 and 1982. This ostensibly positive picture is a quantitative one. However, performances of educational systems have to be measured in terms of the quality of output as well. Two indicators that are useful herein are those concerning drop-out and repetition, 16/ and they are considered in the chapter on regional perspectives below. It should also be noted that though primary education statistics do not usually apply to the 15-24 age group, primary education does have a major impact upon youth, because it is one crucial determinant of their attainments at the secondary and tertiary levels.

In the developed countries, the period 1960-1982 saw the continued provision of universal primary education; the nearing of the goal for universal secondary education; and considerable increases in enrolment for third-level education. However, for many developing countries, the goal of universal education at the first level has still not been attained. Primary education enrolment for the whole group of developing countries has, nonetheless, more than doubled, from 216 million in 1960 to 449 million in 1982. Enrolment in secondary education has also grown, at a rate of 7.9 per cent in 1960-1970, 8.4 per cent in 1970-1975, and less rapidly, at 4.1 per cent in 1975-1982. The absolute numbers in secondary education were 37 million in 1960, rising to 156 million in 1982. Similar rates of growth have been registered in enrolment for tertiary education in the developing countries: absolute figures of about 4 million in 1960 rose to 20 million in 1982, at growth rates of 7 per cent in the 1960s, 11.7 per cent in 1970-1975, and 7.2 per cent in 1975-1982. Worldwide rates of growth, for the same periods, were 7.9, 7.0 and 3.3 per cent.

With regard to female enrolment, the last two decades have seen worldwide increases that match the growth of male enrolment. 17/ This is an encouraging trend. However, it should not be seen in isolation. The absolute number of

Table 7. Public expenditure on education, 1960-1981 (millions of United States dollars at current market prices) and as a percentage of GNP

Regional/country grouping	1960		1965		1970		1975		1980		1981	
	Millions of dollars	As percentage of GNP	Millions of dollars	As percentage of GNP	Millions of dollars	As percentage of GNP	Millions of dollars	As percentage of GNP	Millions of dollars	As percentage of GNP	Millions of dollars	As percentage of GNP
World total a/	51 520	3.6	95 810	4.8	159 552	5.4	332 127	5.7	611 875	5.7	627 535	5.7
Developed countries	47 061	3.9	88 041	5.1	146 984	5.7	294 757	6.0	530 215	6.1	535 808	6.1
Developing countries a/	4 459	2.3	7 769	2.8	12 568	3.3	37 370	3.9	81 660	4.0	91 727	4.1
Africa	975	2.7	1 737	3.5	3 138	4.1	8 431	4.6	19 517	4.5	20 137	4.7
North America	21 203	3.9	40 049	5.4	71 839	6.7	113 288	6.6	200 130	6.9	221 168	6.9
Latin America and the Caribbean	1 674	2.1	3 310	3.1	5 537	3.3	14 277	3.5	32 676	4.0	40 342	4.2
Asia a/	3 771	2.9	6 998	3.2	12 551	3.5	43 305	4.8	95 886	5.0	103 943	5.0
Europe and USSR	23 294	3.9	42 644	5.0	64 502	5.2	145 833	5.8	253 269	5.6	230 038	5.6
Oceania	603	2.9	1 071	3.6	1 984	4.3	6 993	6.2	10 396	5.9	11 907	5.9
Arab States b/	572	3.4	984	2.5	1 798	5.1	8 436	5.9	17 757	4.6	19 040	4.6

Source: United Nations Educational, Scientific and Cultural Organization, A Summary Statistical Review of Education in the World, 1960-1982 (ED/BIE/CONFINTED 39/Rep.1, 12 July 1984).

a/ Not including China, Democratic Kampuchea, Democratic People's Republic of Korea, Lao People's Democratic Republic, Lebanon, Mongolia and Viet Nam.

b/ Data for the Arab States (not including Lebanon) are also included in Africa and Asia.

Table 8. GNP per inhabitant and public expenditure on education, 1960-1981
(United States dollars at current market prices and index 1960=1)

Region/country grouping	Year	GNP per inhabitant (dollars)	Public expenditure on education		GNP per inhabitant (index)	Public expenditure on education	
			Per inhabitant (dollars)	Per pupil (dollars)		Per inhabitant (index)	Per pupil (index)
World total a/	1960	617	23	162	1.0	1.0	1.0
	1965	792	38	235	1.3	1.7	1.5
	1970	1 070	57	334	1.7	2.5	2.1
	1975	1 917	109	600	3.1	4.7	3.7
	1980	3 217	183	973	5.2	8.0	6.0
	1981	3 229	184	962	5.2	8.0	5.9
Developed countries	1960	1 264	49	264	1.0	1.0	1.0
	1965	1 689	86	421	1.3	1.8	1.6
	1970	2 422	137	649	1.9	2.8	2.5
	1975	4 377	264	1 250	3.5	5.4	4.7
	1980	7 499	457	2 283	5.9	9.3	8.6
	1981	7 482	458	2 272	5.9	9.3	8.6
Developing countries a/	1960	148	3	32	1.0	1.0	1.0
	1965	183	5	39	1.2	1.7	1.2
	1970	224	7	50	1.5	2.3	1.6
	1975	495	19	118	3.3	6.3	3.7
	1980	937	37	206	6.3	12.3	6.4
	1981	1 007	41	220	6.8	13.7	6.9
Africa	1960	130	4	47	1.0	1.0	1.0
	1965	161	6	59	1.2	1.5	1.3
	1970	218	9	81	1.7	2.3	1.7
	1975	453	21	156	3.5	5.3	3.3
	1980	920	42	246	7.1	10.5	5.2
	1981	899	42	240	6.9	10.5	5.1

continued

Table 8 (continued)

Region/country grouping	Year	GNP per inhabitant (dollars)	Public expenditure on education		GNP per inhabitant (index)	Public expenditure on education	
			Per inhabitant (dollars)	Per pupil (dollars)		Per inhabitant (index)	Per pupil (index)
North America	1960	2 760	107	447	1.0	1.0	1.0
	1965	3 484	187	701	1.3	1.7	1.6
	1970	4 761	317	1 138	1.7	3.0	2.5
	1975	7 270	479	1 758	2.6	4.5	3.9
	1980	11 639	808	3 363	4.2	7.6	7.5
	1981	12 892	884	3 523	4.7	8.3	7.9
Latin America and the Caribbean	1960	367	8	54	1.0	1.0	1.0
	1965	429	13	79	1.2	1.6	1.5
	1970	597	20	99	1.6	2.5	1.8
	1975	1 256	44	198	3.4	5.5	3.7
	1980	2 251	90	376	6.1	11.3	7.0
	1981	2 555	108	450	7.0	13.5	8.3
Asia a/	1960	139	4	33	1.0	1.0	1.0
	1965	207	7	46	1.5	1.8	1.4
	1970	297	10	69	2.1	2.5	2.1
	1975	670	32	199	4.8	8.0	6.0
	1980	1 288	64	368	9.3	16.0	11.2
	1981	1 372	68	381	9.9	17.0	11.5
Europe and USSR	1960	936	37	226	1.0	1.0	1.0
	1965	1 265	63	346	1.4	1.7	1.5
	1970	1 787	92	479	1.9	2.5	2.1
	1975	3 497	201	1 043	3.7	5.4	4.6
	1980	6 055	339	1 836	6.5	9.2	8.1
	1981	5 459	307	1 670	5.8	8.3	7.4

continued

Table 8 (continued)

Region/country grouping	Year	GNP per inhabitant (dollars)	Public expenditure on education		GNP per inhabitant (index)	Public expenditure on education	
			Per inhabitant (dollars)	Per pupil (dollars)		Per inhabitant (index)	Per pupil (index)
Oceania	1960	1 322	38	204	1.0	1.0	1.0
	1965	1 697	62	300	1.3	1.6	1.5
	1970	2 377	103	476	1.8	2.7	2.3
	1975	5 323	331	1 545	4.0	8.7	7.6
	1980	7 853	460	2 190	5.9	12.1	10.7
	1981	8 714	518	2 500	6.6	13.6	12.3
Arab States b/	1960	192	7	70	1.0	1.0	1.0
	1965	385	10	80	2.0	1.4	1.1
	1970	299	15	113	1.6	2.1	1.6
	1975	1 040	62	374	5.4	8.9	5.3
	1980	2 395	110	596	12.5	15.7	8.5
	1981	2 502	115	607	13.0	16.4	8.7

Source: United Nations Educational, Scientific and Cultural Organization, A Summary Statistical Review of Education in the World, 1960-1982 (ED/BIE/CONFINTED 39/Rep.1, 12 July 1984).

a/ Not including China, Democratic Kampuchea, Democratic People's Republic of Korea, Lao People's Democratic Republic, Lebanon, Mongolia and Viet Nam.

b/ Data for the Arab States (not including Lebanon) are also included in Africa and Asia.

females not enrolled in regular education is still much greater than that of males. For the developed countries and the Latin American region, parity between the sexes with regard to first and second levels of education was achieved by 1960. This trend continues, and, in the developed countries, disparity has virtually disappeared; even at the tertiary level. The picture is less bright in the developing countries, where large disparities are still manifest at all three educational levels.

Between 1960 and 1982, there was a positive global trend of reduced pupil-teacher ratios, resulting from increases in the number of teachers, at all levels, outpacing the growth of enrolment. For primary education, the world pupil-teacher ratio dropped from 30 in 1960 to 28 in 1982. In 1980, however, 84 countries had ratios that were greater than the global average of 28. In secondary education, the ratio dropped from 20 to 18, though 74 countries had ratios higher than the global average of 18 in 1980. For tertiary education, the world average dropped from 14 in 1960 to 12 in 1982 (table 9). 18/ The participation of females in the teaching profession has

Table 9. Pupil-teacher ratios, by level of education, 1960-1982

Region/country grouping	Year	First level	Second level	Third level
World total	1980	27	17	13
	1982	27	18	12
World total (not including China)	1960	30	20	14
	1965	30	18	14
	1970	29	17	14
	1975	28	17	14
	1980	28	17	13
	1982	28	18	12
Developed countries	1960	26	21	14
	1965	23	17	14
	1970	22	16	14
	1975	21	15	14
	1980	19	15	13
	1982	20	15	13
Developing countries (not including China)	1960	36	19	16
	1965	38	19	16
	1970	37	19	15
	1975	35	20	15
	1980	34	20	14
	1982	33	21	11
Africa	1960	40	19	17
	1965	41	21	16
	1970	41	24	14
	1975	40	24	16
	1980	36	21	15
	1982	37	23	14

continued

Table 9 (continued)

Region/country grouping	Year	First level	Second level	Third level
Latin America and the Caribbean	1960	34	11	8
	1965	34	10	8
	1970	35	10	10
	1975	28	15	11
	1980	29	16	11
	1982	29	16	11
North America	1960	27	27	13
	1965	27	21	14
	1970	23	20	15
	1975	20	18	17
	1980	17	17	14
	1982	15	18	13
Asia (not including China)	1960	36	22	16
	1965	39	23	17
	1970	36	21	16
	1975	36	21	15
	1980	35	20	16
	1982	35	21	12
Europe and USSR	1960	24	17	15
	1965	22	14	15
	1970	21	14	13
	1975	20	14	13
	1980	19	14	12
	1982	19	14	12
Oceania	1960	30	24	16
	1965	27	20	15
	1970	27	19	15
	1975	23	16	13
	1980	22	15	14
	1982	22	15	14
Arab States a/	1960	37	17	18
	1965	36	20	21
	1970	35	22	18
	1975	32	22	19
	1980	30	20	17
	1982	30	20	17

Source: United Nations Educational, Scientific and Cultural Organization, A Summary Statical Review of Education in the World, 1960-1982 (ED/BIE/CONFINTED 39/Rep.1, 12 July 1984).

a/ Data for the Arab States are also included in Africa and Asia.

shown some changes in the last two decades. Female teachers continue to
dominate primary and pre-primary education: they constituted a global average
of 56 per cent of all teachers at this level in 1960, and the percentage was
the same in 1982. In secondary education, female teachers have registered a
worldwide increase, from 36 per cent in 1960 to 44 per cent in 1982. 18/

The numbers of students pursuing their tertiary education abroad continues
to increase. In 1981, the number was estimated to be over 1 million, representing
an increase of 14.5 per cent over the figure for 1978. Over 70 per cent of
the 1981 world total were in five major host countries: France, Germany,
Federal Republic of, United Kingdom, United States and USSR. 19/ However,
international student exchange has not been insulated from the baneful
influence of recession. Sharp increases in fees, and restrictive quotas for
foreign students in some host developed countries, coupled with the paucity of
foreign exchange in the developing countries, have resulted in a decrease in
students going from the latter to the former countries. A positive dimension
of this situation has been the rapid expansion of tertiary-level institutions
in the developing regions, particularly Africa and Asia. 20/ A related issue,
the cultural relevance of education, is treated below.

On the general indicator of literacy in the world, there has been
considerable progress in recent years, and projections indicate that this
upward trend will continue. 21/ In 1970, some 32.9 per cent of the world
population was illiterate (27.7 per cent males and 38 per cent females). The
comparable figures for 1985 were projected at 26.8 per cent total (21.5 per
cent males and 32 per cent females), and for the year 2000 at 21.5 per cent
total (17 per cent males and 26 per cent females) (table 10). 22/ However,
these statistics are for the 15-plus age group, and do not provide a clear
picture of the situation of the 15-24 group. It is clear, though, that behind
this apparently optimistic statistical picture lies the sombre fact that the
last people to benefit from educational development are those who need it the
most: rural populations, the urban poor, minority groups, and, in many
countries, girls and women 23/ - in short, the people who have been categorized
here as marginalized. Their situation has often been hamstrung by the
generally distorting effects of scarcity in the labour market in relation to
supply. As more and more young people acquire the requisite qualifications
for jobs, the number of these jobs does not increase proportionately. A way
out of the situation, for many employers, has been to progressively raise the
requirements of educational credentials required for the job in question. The
negative aspect of this process has been that young people who have recently
acquired some degree of education are pushed out of the job market by others
who have a higher education and have to shift to occupations of a lower rank.
There is thus a generalized downward movement in which the lowest ranks - those
with rudimentary education - are driven out of the formal job market. A
solution will have to be found in better educational coverage for marginal
groups of youth, so that they may complete for jobs more effectively. Only by
means such as these will the rigid vicious circle between education deficiency
and poverty be broken.

Table 10. Illiteracy in the world and major regions, age 15-plus, 1970-2000 a/

Region/country grouping	Sex	1970 Millions	1970 Per cent	1980 Millions	1980 Per cent	1985 Millions	1985 Per cent	1990 Millions	1990 Per cent	2000 Millions	2000 Per cent
World total											
Population	MF	2 309.8		2 879.2		3 203.2		3 545.7		4 241.7	
	M	1 145.3		1 431.9		1 596.2		1 770.2		2 122.9	
	F	1 164.5		1 447.3		1 607.0		1 775.5		2 118.7	
Literates	MF	1 549.6		2 055.1		2 345.9		2 663.6		3 329.8	
	M	827.7		1 098.6		1 253.8		1 420.4		1 762.7	
	F	721.9		956.5		1 092.2		1 243.2		1 567.1	
Illiterates	MF	760.2		824.1		857.2		882.1		911.9	
	M	317.6		333.3		342.4		349.9		360.2	
	F	442.6		490.9		514.8		532.2		551.6	
Illiteracy rate	MF		32.9		28.6		26.8		24.9		21.5
	M		27.7		23.3		21.5		19.8		17.0
	F		38.0		33.9		32.0		30.0		26.0
Developed countries b/											
Population	MF	784.5		889.7		931.0		967.4		1 039.7	
	M	370.1		423.8		445.6		465.0		504.4	
	F	414.4		465.9		485.4		502.4		535.4	
Literates	MF	755.8		867.3		911.2		950.1			
	M	359.2		415.5		438.2		458.5			
	F	396.6		451.8		473.0		491.6			
Illiterates	MF	28.7		22.5		19.8		17.4			
	M	10.9		8.3		7.4		6.5			
	F	17.8		14.1		12.4		10.8			
Illiteracy rate	MF		3.7		2.5		2.1		1.8		
	M		3.0		2.0		1.7		1.4		
	F		4.3		3.0		2.6		2.2		

continued

Table 10 (continued)

Region/country grouping	Sex	1970 Millions	1970 Per cent	1980 Millions	1980 Per cent	1985 Millions	1985 Per cent	1990 Millions	1990 Per cent	2000 Millions	2000 Per cent
Developing countries											
Population	MF	1 525.3		1 989.5		2 272.2		2 578.3		3 201.9	
	M	775.2		1 008.0		1 150.6		1 305.2		1 618.6	
	F	750.1		981.4		1 121.5		1 273.1		1 583.4	
Literates	MF	793.8		1 188.1		1 434.6		1 713.7		2 304.0	
	M	468.5		683.1		815.6		961.8		1 263.7	
	F	325.3		504.9		619.1		751.8		1 040.4	
Illiterates	MF	731.4		801.4		837.5		864.6		897.9	
	M	306.7		324.9		335.0		343.4		354.9	
	F	424.7		476.5		502.5		521.2		543.0	
Illiteracy rate	MF		48.0		40.3		36.9		33.5		28.0
	M		39.6		32.2		29.1		26.3		21.9
	F		56.6		48.5		44.8		40.9		34.3
Africa											
Population	MF	196.6		259.1		299.6		348.0		478.5	
	M	96.1		127.3		147.4		171.5		236.4	
	F	100.5		131.8		152.2		176.5		242.1	
Literates	MF	56.9		102.9		137.7		183.1		310.1	
	M	37.4		64.3		83.7		107.7		173.3	
	F	19.4		38.5		54.1		75.3		136.8	
Illiterates	MF	139.7		156.2		161.9		164.9		168.4	
	M	58.6		62.9		63.8		63.7		63.0	
	F	81.1		93.3		98.1		101.2		105.4	
Illiteracy rate	MF		71.1		60.3		54.0		47.4		35.2
	M		61.0		49.5		43.3		37.2		26.7
	F		80.7		70.8		64.5		57.3		43.5

continued

Table 10 (continued)

Region/country grouping	Sex	1970 Millions	1970 Per cent	1980 Millions	1980 Per cent	1985 Millions	1985 Per cent	1990 Millions	1990 Per cent	2000 Millions	2000 Per cent
Latin America and the Caribbean											
Population	MF	162.8		219.0		252.5		288.3		369.6	
	M	81.2		109.1		125.8		143.7		184.1	
	F	81.6		109.9		126.7		144.7		185.5	
Literates	MF	118.4		174.7		208.9		246.1		331.2	
	M	61.6		89.5		106.5		124.9		166.8	
	F	56.8		85.1		102.4		121.2		164.4	
Illiterates	MF	44.4		44.3		43.6		42.2		38.4	
	M	19.6		19.6		19.2		18.7		17.3	
	F	24.8		24.8		24.3		23.5		21.1	
Illiteracy rate	MF		27.3		20.2		17.3		14.6		10.4
	M		24.2		17.9		15.3		13.0		9.4
	F		30.4		22.5		19.2		16.2		11.4
North America b/											
Population	MF	162.0		190.9		201.4		209.6		233.1	
	M	78.2		92.2		97.4		101.4		114.3	
	F	83.8		98.7		104.0		108.2		118.9	
Literates	MF	159.8									
	M	77.1									
	F	82.7									
Illiterates	MF	2.2									
	M	1.2									
	F	1.1									
Illiteracy rate	MF		1.4								
	M		1.5								
	F		1.3								

continued

Table 10 (continued)

Region/country grouping	Sex	1970 Millions	1970 Per cent	1980 Millions	1980 Per cent	1985 Millions	1985 Per cent	1990 Millions	1990 Per cent	2000 Millions	2000 Per cent
Asia											
Population	MF	1 257.8		1 617.2		1 833.4		2 063.8		2 488.6	
	M	642.4		823.2		932.7		1 049.7		1 264.3	
	F	615.4		794.0		900.7		1 014.1		1 224.3	
Literates	MF	706.9		1 012.9		1 199.4		1 404.4		1 795.5	
	M	412.2		579.2		679.7		787.8		988.8	
	F	294.7		433.7		519.7		616.5		806.7	
Illiterates	MF	550.9		604.3		634.0		659.4		693.0	
	M	230.2		244.0		253.0		261.8		275.5	
	F	320.7		360.3		381.0		397.5		417.5	
Illiteracy rate	MF		43.8		37.4		34.6		31.9		27.8
	M		35.8		29.6		27.1		24.9		21.8
	F		52.1		45.4		42.3		39.2		34.1
Europe (including USSR) b/											
Population	MF	517.4		576.8		598.7		617.0		649.9	
	M	240.8		272.0		284.1		294.5		312.9	
	F	276.7		304.9		314.6		322.5		336.9	
Literates	MF	496.1		560.6		584.8		605.0			
	M	233.5		266.7		279.6		290.6			
	F	262.6		293.9		305.2		314.4			
Illiterates	MF	21.3		16.2		13.9		12.0			
	M	7.3		5.3		4.5		3.9			
	F	14.0		10.9		9.4		8.1			
Illiteracy rate	MF		4.1		2.8		2.3		1.9		
	M		3.0		1.9		1.6		1.3		
	F		5.1		3.6		3.0		2.5		

continued

Table 10 (continued)

Region/country grouping	Sex	1970 Millions	1970 Per cent	1980 Millions	1980 Per cent	1985 Millions	1985 Per cent	1990 Millions	1990 Per cent	2000 Millions	2000 Per cent
Oceania											
Population	MF	13.1		16.1		17.5		19.0		21.9	
	M	6.6		8.1		8.8		9.5		11.0	
	F	6.5		8.0		8.7		9.5		10.9	
Literates	MF	11.6		14.5		16.0		17.5		20.5	
	M	5.9		7.4		8.1		8.9		10.4	
	F	5.7		7.1		7.8		8.6		10.0	
Illiterates	MF	1.5		1.6		1.6		1.5		1.5	
	M	0.7		0.7		0.7		0.6		0.5	
	F	0.8		0.9		0.9		0.9		0.9	
Illiteracy rate c/	MF		11.5		9.7		8.9		8.1		6.6
	M		10.8		8.5		7.6		6.7		5.0
	F		12.2		10.8		10.2		9.6		8.3
Arab States c/											
Population	MF	67.1		91.9		107.7		125.3		171.7	
	M	33.4		46.1		54.1		63.1		86.7	
	F	33.7		45.8		53.6		62.2		85.1	
Literates	MF	18.3		34.8		46.9		61.8		102.7	
	M	13.5		23.9		31.0		39.5		61.8	
	F	4.9		10.9		15.9		22.2		41.0	
Illiterates	MF	48.8		57.1		60.8		63.6		69.0	
	M	19.9		22.2		23.1		23.6		24.9	
	F	28.8		34.9		37.7		40.0		44.1	
Illiteracy rate c/	MF		72.7		62.1		56.5		50.7		40.2
	M		59.7		48.2		42.6		37.4		28.7
	F		85.6		76.1		70.4		64.3		51.9

Source: United Nations Educational, Scientific and Cultural Organization, A Summary Statistical Review of Education in the World, 1960-1982 (ED/BIE/CONFINTED 39/Rep.1, 12 July 1984).

a/ As assessed in 1982.

b/ Illiteracy projections are not shown for years when the illiteracy rates for all 5-year age-groups were less than 5 per cent.

c/ Data for Arab States are also included in Africa and Asia.

Yet, this is by no means a certainty. The powerful nineteenth century shibboleth about education being the greatest equalizer seems increasingly dubious. In many cases, education now appears, rather, as an instrument by means of which distinctions are often instilled, and existing differences often reproduced. There appears to be a growing recognition that even if education does make the poor more competent, it does not thereby eradicate their poverty. Further, the contribution of education to economic growth is not always a positive one. There is not necessarily a direct correlation between the amount of formal education and economic success, at either the individual or the aggregate level. 24/ Thus do many countries face a problem of "over-education", particularly in the form of a surplus of university graduates. Thus also do youth unemployment figures, in many parts of the world, and despite ever-increasing formal education, climb inexorably higher.

The problem here is a generic one, and appears to apply to many kinds of societies: the increasingly apparent disjunction between formal schooling and the world of work, as was noted above. All over the world, efforts have been made to integrate work into the school curriculum and to break the long established dominance of the academic subjects. 25/ The essential thrust of these efforts has been to bridge the gaps between schools and the communities within which they exist, and at meeting the needs of the labour market more directly, by pointing more young people towards expanding industries and occupations, and away from those sectors that are saturated in terms of manpower. Yet the disjunction remains, and continues to be felt everywhere: in the developed market economy countries, the centrally planned economies, and the developing countries. The problem is quintessentially one of quality, not quantity, and the critique appears to hinge upon three issues: first, the concern about the general intellectual capabilities of school and university leavers; second, the belief that their range of knowledge is not sufficient for them to enter employment; and, third, the complaints that young people have a lackadaisical attitude to employment. Past experience of efforts to narrow the work-school gap indicates that it is difficult to simulate work conditions in the classroom, as well as to treat productive work as one subject among others. In cognizance of this caveat, several new initiatives appear to be in train.

One of these, prevalent in industrial countries with centrally planned economies, is the school patronage system. 26/ This implies that a secondary school is put under the patronage of one or more industrial enterprise, the relationship and tasks of the two institutions being formalized in a bilateral contract. The patron enterprise provides the school with permanent technical and financial assistance; the students' productive activities fulfil the enterprise's need for skilled manpower. The system is integrated into the general secondary education programme and is linked to the production system of the country in question. As, however, the experiment is a relatively recent one, its success is difficult to measure at this early stage.

In the developed market economies, there is evidence of a shift in emphasis from training in formal schools to training in the work environment, either within the firms themselves, or within independent schools and colleges established by interested enterprises. 27/ The rationale for this appears to be the perceived failure of the formal education system to keep pace with the very rapid technological advance that is manifest in these societies. Related to this is the fact that the social cost of training shifts from the individual taxpayer to its eventual user - the company or enterprise in question. The general configuration which emerges seems particularly apposite during recessionary or low-growth periods: both Governments and educational institutions, in view of budgetary constraints, would appear to welcome the

shift of the training burden towards the eventual user. Again, it is too
early to make an assessment of these tendencies. If they do continue to
spread, however, it seems likely that they will engender major changes: the
curricula of formal schools might change towards the provision of general
skills, rather than specific capabilities; and there might be a decrease in
the length of formal training, in conjunction with a corresponding increase of
the later-in-life educational component. 28/

    Many developing countries have seen various initiatives to come to grips
with the problem of a more productive interaction between education and work.
However, scarcities of resources, as well as difficulties in implementation,
qualify these efforts. Problems here are much larger, and consequently
dispersed over a wider social area. A particularly difficult question is that
of cultural relevance: the relationship between education and the cultural
identity of society. This relationship is not always a harmonious one,
because, in the case of many developing countries, the educational system
continues to reflect its colonial heritage, and this is often at odds with the
contemporary cultural needs and values of the society in question. Perhaps
the most widespread difficulty here is the one associated with language, and
the difficulties of replacing a colonially inherited language with a different
national language. The linguistic medium is one through which the essence of
culture can permeate into education, thereby making the latter more relevant
to social needs and norms. Some countries have tried to solve the problem by
changing the language, but not the subject matter, of education. Others have
attempted reforms that modernize language teaching in a bilingual context, but
again, do little to change the content of educational programmes. There are
several other difficulties, often of a wider political and social provenance,
associated with the policy of promoting national languages. Many of these
become manifest in those societies that are internally differentiated along
ethnic and linguistic lines.

Employment

    Another problem which has an almost universal dimension, across the major
regions, is that of youth employment, and the related issues of unemployment,
underemployment and migration. The connection between the economic recession
and the lack of jobs available, especially to young people, is clear and well
established. What is not so well documented, however, is the situation
prevailing with regard to the actual search for work, as well as the real
nature of that work itself. In the present decade, it has become evident that
these problems loom large, in reality as well as in the consciousness of young
people. Environmental hazards, physical risk, psychological and cultural
alienation, economic marginalization - these are some of the issues that are
subsumed within the larger question of the nature of work that is available to
youth. Statistics on employment, given the complexity of the problem, are
often inadequate. Little information is available, for instance, on the work
patterns of young people in the informal sectors of the economy. Unpaid
labour, mostly provided by young women, is omitted from official statistics.
Economic activities of other marginalized youth groups are not categorized or
quantified. In the less developed regions of the world, and particularly in
the cities and shanty towns around them, young people work in a variety of
occupational categories: sweat-shop workers, self-employed artisans, service
technicians, street vendors, itinerant salesmen, casual wage labour, refuse
collectors, prostitutes, beggars, and the huge personal service sector. Far
too many young people's lives are characterized by an immense volatility of
occupation, and by the fact that the process whereby they try to become
workers is often not consummated at all. Any effort directed at integrating
young people more closely into the world of work must therefore be informed by
an adequate appreciation of these situations.

A general demographic profile of the global youth population was drawn in
chapter II. With regard to employment, the number of economically active
young people in the world has to be considered. Table 11 provides these
figures, showing worldwide distribution as well as the difference between
adolescents and young adults. In 1980, there were 475 million economically
active young people in the world, which means more than one young person out
of two. Of this total, only 24 per cent (110 million) were in the developed
countries, as against 365 million in the developing countries, three quarters
of them in Asia. Projections for the year 2000 indicate over-all increases in
the numbers of active youth. There will be a significant decline in the
developed regions, especially Western Europe, North America and the USSR, but
this will be balanced by substantial increases in all the developing regions,
with the exception of China.

Table 11. Active youth population: distribution and trend by age

Region and year	15-19 years old		20-24 years old	
	Total (millions)	As a percentage of the age group	Total (millions)	As a percentage of the age group
World				
1960	149	57	180	71
1980	198	44	277	68
2000	191	34	338	66
More developed regions				
1960	38	56	57	75
1980	38	40	72	75
2000	29	33	65	75
Less developed regions				
1960	111	57	123	69
1980	160	45	205	66
2000	162	35	273	64

Source: International Labour Organisation, Report of the Director-General,
1982 (Geneva, 1982).

The figures also show sharp increases in the activity rate of youth from
one age group to the other. In 1980, one out of two adolescents was active.
However, as the process of their integration into the educational and training
structure continues, the proportion of those who are active is likely to drop
by the year 2000: from 40 to 33 per cent in the developed regions, and from
45 to 35 per cent in the developing regions. More than two out of three young
adults, by contrast, were active in 1980, with participation rates of 75 per
cent in developed areas, and 66 per cent in less developed areas. In the year
2000, these rates are projected to remain the same in the former, and drop
marginally, to 64 per cent, in the latter areas. Differences between
adolescent and young adult participation rates can be attributed, in the main,
to the level of development in the region, and to differences in school
attendance. More adolescents than young adults attend schools and training
courses, all over the world. However, more adolescents in the developing
countries are forced to leave school early because of economic pressures.

Another significant factor is the difference between male and female activity rates. With the major exception of adolescents in China, worldwide figures for 1982 showed a higher proportion of men than women. Further, the gap tends to widen with age, except in the case of the USSR, where the activity rate of young adult women was extremely high (80 per cent). The gap was widest in the developing countries, excepting China: the young adult male activity rate was generally 85 to 90 per cent, whereas the rate for young adult females was less than half of this. In the developed countries, the gap was less; so also was the young adult male activity rate. With regard to adolescents, the picture is similar: participation rates of adolescent boys were higher in the developing than in the developed countries, unlike those of girls. 29/

These figures, conflated with the general demographic data in chapter II, together point to the fact that the problems caused by the influx of young people to the employment market are far more acute in the developing countries than in the developed ones. In 1980, for instance, four times more adolescents, and almost three times more young adults, were working, or looking for work, in the former than in the latter countries. In the year 2000, the number of young active persons will rise by almost 20 per cent in the developing countries; in the developed countries, it will decline by 15 per cent. These countries are, in the long run, liable to be confronted with a relative shortage of young workers. The developing countries, on the other hand, will have to continue trying to find useful work for an ever-increasing and youthful labour force.

Any general examination of youth employment upon the global level must begin with the caveat that youth is not a monolithic and homogeneous social block, but is made up of many diverse sub-categories of people. Thus, different kinds of young people approach work with a variety of different aspirations. Differences from one region, country and locality to another are added to differences between sub-groups, between rural and urban youth, rich and poor youth, literate and illiterate youth, national and immigrant youth, male and female youth, adolescents and young adults. All young people, however, are products of their economic, social and cultural environment, which determines their socialization. The context of this socialization differs enormously; therefore, a distinction must be made between the problems facing youth in different kinds of societies, in the developed and developing regions of the world.

Distinctions notwithstanding, a global nexus can still be established, particularly in regard to young people's attitude towards, and expectations from, the world of work. Certain negative reactions on the part of some young people are particularly important because they are often symptomatic of the disaffection of many towards their work. They also provide grist for the critique that many employers adopt against younger sections of the labour force. One reaction that is prevalent among marginalized sub-groups of youth - those from poor rural communities for instance - is the resignation, even fatalism, that sometimes characterizes their attitudes to work and employment. This often happens because the enthusiasm and realism with which the search for employment begins is impossible to maintain in the teeth of consistent rejection, or even consistent under-valuing of ability. These reactions may characterize only a small minority, but, as pointed out above, they are often the extreme manifestations of a more general predicament: rejection, in one form or another, is a compelling reality for far too many young people in the world.

A less extreme, but more prevalent, reaction is the ostensibly lackadaisical attitude that many young people are supposed to have towards employment and work. This usually results from a certain kind of apathy and passivity, engendered by young people being dissatisfied with their work, uninterested in their jobs, and performing them as unavoidable chores. A serious dichotomy ensues, because these people begin to perceive their personal lives and their work as two quite different things, and there is often tension between them. Many young people seek to bridge the gap by drifting from one job to another, hoping to find their vocation, and thus end the dichotomy. If there is any success herein, it is qualified by the young person concerned acquiring the pejorative label of being a "drifter". In both the developed market economies and the centrally planned economies, various studies have shown that more than one worker in three under the age of 25 changes jobs at least once. 30/ Even worse, a recent international survey showed that 70 per cent of young people were not employed in the kind of work for which they were trained, and in which they began their working life. 31/ Negative responses may also be reflected in absenteeism, a lack of conscientiousness, low productivity, and even bad workmanship. While these are by no means general phenomena, they collectively suggest the existence of a widespread malaise that demands attention.

Unemployment and underemployment together constitute a malaise which is so prevalent among young people that there are very few parts of the world where finding a satisfactory job and making a good start in working life is not something of a problem. General employment is in any case a major problem in many parts of the world, and the young are particularly vulnerable to it. Table 12 shows how major a factor youth unemployment is. In the 28 countries listed, the young account for over half the total unemployed in 11 countries, and in only 4 countries do they represent less than a third. Even though these figures show such a high level of youth unemployment, they are still only the tip of the iceberg. Statistics, even when they are available, and they often are not in the developing countries, say little about the problem of hidden unemployment, or the mechanisms of rejection that drive so many young people into a fatalism of being jobless. They say little, too, about the phenomenon, widespread in the developing countries, of the underemployment of young people who can only find odd jobs with low productivity and a pittance for wages, whether in rural areas or in the urban informal sector. While we may refer to these people as underemployed, this category is not usually used in official statistics. They are therefore treated as unemployed young people. And yet, they are not so, because they do work, but in areas that are denied official statistical cognizance: the household, the sweat-shop, the street, the garbage-dump, the brothel. "Unemployment", then, often appears to be merely a managerial category constructed for bureaucratic purposes, according to bureaucratic criteria, and covering all those who are not counted by government agencies as working for, say, more than 40 paid hours a week. 32/

Table 12. Unemployed youth as a percentage of total unemployed,
selected countries, 1980

Country	Percentage	Country	Percentage
Thailand a/	73.9	Canada	47.1
Syrian Arab Republic b/	69.9	Israel	46.6
India b/	67.2	United States	45.7

continued

Table 12 (continued)

Country	Percentage	Country	Percentage
Barbados	66.2	Netherlands	44.7
Italy	62.4	Sweden	42.4
Ghana	60.4	United Kingdom	42.2
Venezuela b/	58.2	France	42.1
Singapore	58.0	Belgium	38.0
Spain b/	57.5	Norway	35.9
Australia	55.9	Finland	33.9
Philippines b/	54.9	Denmark b/	27.9
Turkey b/	48.6	Germany, Federal Republic of	27.3
Korea, Republic of	48.6	Switzerland	23.5
Portugal	47.4	Japan	21.9

Source: International Labour Organisation, Report of the Director-General, 1982 (Geneva, 1982).

a/ 1978.

b/ 1979.

Whether accorded official recognition or not, there is little doubt that unemployment and underemployment among young people is a major problem in most parts of the world. It is not only a problem for young people per se, but also for every community and society of which they are a part. The problems and consequences for young people themselves have been elaborated throughout this study. In modern societies, the acquisition of a stable and secure job has an almost ritualistic quality: it is a social imprimatur of adult status. The fact that it is denied to an ever-increasing number of young people - about 40 per cent of all young people in the mainly market-oriented developed and developing countries 33/ - has menacing implications for the future. The picture becomes even more tenebrous when the social costs of this phenomenon are considered. An unemployed, or chronically underemployed, person has little stake in the established social and political system. He becomes alienated, and perhaps even anti-social. If there are many like him, their collective effect becomes progressively disruptive. The cumulative impact is the loss of a vital resource for development. Progressive losses could engender a regressive configuration. The advent of a generation without adequate skills or productive work experience could disrupt the process of renewal of the labour force, and future economic growth could be seriously jeopardized.

Given the diverse economic, social and cultural conditions that prevail in different parts of the world, and the consequently different facets of youth employment problems, remedies have been variegated. In broad terms, however, these measures fall into four major categories, and most countries have resorted to them, in varying degrees: fiscal, budgetary and monetary measures aimed at over-all demand; more selective action in order to aid particularly badly hit regions or sectors; labour market policies consisting of better placement arrangements, measures to increase labour mobility, development of vocational guidance, training and retraining facilities; and specific aids to youth employment. 34/ In the context of these general policy measures, the following paragraphs provide a conspectus of the youth employment situation in different parts of the world.

In the 24 developed market economy countries of the Organisation for Economic Co-operation and Development (OECD), there were roughly 35 million people unemployed at the end of 1983. 35/ At the end of 1980, youth unemployment figures for those countries stood at 6.5 million, compared with 1 million a decade earlier. There has been a rapid deterioration in the ratio between adult and youth unemployment, which was in the order of one to three in 1980. 36/ Expressed another way, in the early 1980s, persons under 25 years of age who were available for and willing to work had at least twice as many chances of being underemployed as persons over 25. 37/ General characteristics of the employment situation can be expressed in two propositions. First, ten persons out of a hundred were unemployed at the end of 1983. Of the ten persons, five were young, and three of these were young women. Secondly, among the unemployed queueing up for unskilled jobs, the successful applicants will first be adult males (between 25 and 54 years of age); next will come women of the same age; these will be followed by young persons; last will come the minorities - particularly the young among them - and older workers. 38/

Because of the recession and structural shortcomings, the traditional wage-earning sector is less and less able to absorb the young workers coming on to the employment market. As a consequence, these young people frequently start their working lives in marginal sectors, sometimes even outside the organized, regulated and properly protected labour circuit. These activities are sometimes referred to as "moonlighting", "clandestine" employment and "precarious" employment. Such jobs are usually characterized by instability, low wages and a lack of protection. Similar situations prevail with regard to those that are called "discouraged" workers, or involuntary part-time workers, though these phenomena usually occur slightly later in working lives, frequently in latter parts of the young adult stage. Workers who have given up looking for a job because they know from experience that it is not available are known as discouraged workers. Their unemployment cannot thus be regarded as freely chosen. In 1982, the number of discouraged workers in the United States was 1.5 million, which constituted 1.5 per cent of the labour force. Among them was a high proportion of women and Blacks: they accounted for 64 and 30 per cent of the total number, while they made up only 42 and 12 per cent of the total labour force. With regard to involuntary part-time work, another example can be given from the United States. In 1983, there were more than 6.5 million non-agricultural workers involuntarily on part-time schedules, accounting for 6 per cent of the total labour force. 39/

The ever-increasing problems of youth unemployment are attributed to a number of reasons. In general terms, the economic crisis has caused the number of available jobs to level off, or even drop considerably. On the other hand, there has been a simultaneous increase in the demand for employment, reflecting the baby boom of the 1950s and 1960s, combined with the trend towards a higher female participation rate. Even though there is now considerable evidence of economic recovery, the problems of youth unemployment will not disappear merely by dint of it. There appear to be at least three reasons for this, all of which have already been discussed above: the organization and operation of the labour market which makes employers reluctant to hire young workers; the apparently lackadaisical attitude of the young towards employment; and the disjunction between education/training and work.

In the countries with centrally planned economies, youth employment problems are strikingly different. 40/ These countries enjoy full employment and apply in practice the principle of the right to work and of guaranteed work embodied in their constitutions. The problem is thus not one of youth unemployment, but of an increasingly severe shortage of young manpower, due partly to low birth rates, and partly to the very large proportion of young people, especially adolescents, attending school or undergoing training. In the USSR, for instance, the stated annual enterprise labour requirement was more than twice the available labour during the late 1970s. In Poland, job offers exceeded job seekers by more than 300,000 during 1982. 41/ These are particular manifestations of generic problems that occur, from time to time, in all large and multifaceted economies: difficulties of equating the supply of labour with demand. It is possible here to find a feature that appears to be common to both these countries and the developed market economies, despite the profound differences that separate the two. This is the problem of the underutilization of economic and human capacity. In purely economic terms, full employment thus does not always mean that human resources are fully utilized, or that output is at optimal levels.

The fact that demand for young manpower is not matched by supply has created difficulties about the distribution of young workers among different sectors, and their harmonious integration into working life. In the area of agriculture, for instance, there is the problem of "aging" of the labour force. Agriculture has long been a source of supply for other sectors, yet more young workers are now needed to increase productivity in agriculture. The simultaneous growth of new industry creates an equally compelling demand for more young engineers, technicians and other experts. Helping young people find their place in the economy, and keep their first job, is also something of a problem. In the case of qualified young workers, the system provides for automatic and harmonious placement. But for many other young people, the tendency is to start looking for a better job fairly quickly. Thus do many of these countries have a labour turnover that is twice as high among young people under the age of 30. When the economies of these countries undergo structural modifications, there are sometimes difficulties in offering employment to young workers immediately after they finish their education or training. Though they receive cash benefits in these cases, such situations have become more frequent in recent years as a result of economic and financial difficulties in some East European countries.

Since the mid-1970s, employment policies in the USSR and Eastern Europe have concentrated upon the organization and management of labour, a result of shortages and growing rigidities in the labour force. The problem of youth employment is dealt with by means of a variety of measures, among them specific constitutional provisions, laws and regulations. Higher labour productivity is now seen as a basic prerequisite for accelerated economic growth in the 1980s and beyond. Emphasis is placed upon administrative directives, indirect managerial guidelines, differentiated wage incentives, and improvements in the scope of services and the quality of consumer goods. 41/ Both administrative and managerial employment measures are generally designed to facilitate rapid and orderly changes in the structure of employment. They thereby contribute, along with other specific measures, to solving the problems associated with the employment of young people.

In the developing countries, the problems of youth employment are formidable. All the unemployment and underemployment ratios that are valid for the more developed regions can be doubled, or even trebled, in the case of the developing countries. The number of people with employment problems here is so great that hundreds of millions of jobs are needed immediately. For

instance, at least one third of the active male population has no employment
worthy of the name. 42/ The economic crisis which many of these countries
have encountered in the first half of this decade in the form of stagnant or
falling production, and the austerity measures they have had to adopt in order
to restore external equilibrium, have greatly increased open employment. The
whole structure of employment in most developing countries is, in any case,
very different from that of the developed countries. The distinction between
those who are gainfully employed, and those who are not, is blurred. This is
particularly true in agriculture, and among the large families of the urban
poor. There are substantial differences in support structures for those who
do not, or cannot, earn. There is also, in most developing countries, a large
"informal" sector, which offers many opportunities for casual jobs, but in
conditions where there are few restraints on the exploitation of labour -
particularly women, children, and young people. The cumulative result of all
this is that figures for unemployment, or even for employment, convey a
fragmented, even distorted picture, and are not always sufficient to assess
the situation accurately. Statistics, for those countries where they are
available, are given in table 12. Given these problems of analysis, the
situation can probably be seen most accurately in the context of long-term
changes in the developing world.

The first characteristic of domestic structural transformation in the
developing countries was the decline in the share of agriculture as a proportion of GDP from over 30 to 18 per cent between 1960 and 1980 (table 13).
This is a reflection, at least in part, of a widespread rural employment
crisis in the developing world. Output growth rates have been constrained by
institutional factors, including unequal access to land. In its turn,
sluggish growth has tended to strengthen those very factors making for labour
segmentation and social stratification. Growth, by itself, is unlikely to
solve the problem of rural poverty. For the benefits of growth to filter down
to poorer groups, certain pre-conditions are necessary, for instance a
redistribution of land. In all but a few developing countries, such
pre-conditions are not present. 43/ There is thus a risk that growth will
marginalize the mass of small-holders and labourers, and benefit primarily the
middle and large commercial farmers. In many parts of Africa, for instance,
the transition from customary tenurial systems to commercial agriculture, and
the vast technological differences between the two, seem to be having just
such an effect. Government policies often favour the more progressive farmer;
productivity in the small holding declines, food production falls, and labour
- particularly young labour - migrates to urban areas in search of jobs.

Table 13. Structure of GDP: developing countries, 1960-1980
(In percentages)

Country/group	Agriculture 1960	1980	Industry 1960	1980	Services 1960	1980
All developing countries	31.0	17.3	29.9	38.5	39.1	44.2
Latin America and Caribbean						
Low-income countries	26.2	17.2	27.7	32.0	46.1	51.0
Middle-income countries	16.2	10.0	36.7	39.0	47.1	51.0
China	...	...	...	...	...	...

continued

Table 13 (continued)

Country/group	Agriculture		Industry		Services	
	1960	1980	1960	1980	1960	1980
India	51.0	37.0	19.4	25.0	29.5	38.0
Asia						
Other low-income countries	48.1	33.0	17.5	27.0	34.4	40.0
Middle-income countries	34.8	18.0	21.0	36.0	44.2	46.0
Africa and Middle East						
Low-income countries	54.4	41.0	13.3	17.0	32.4	42.0
Middle-income countries	33.0	20.0	28.3	35.0	38.8	45.0
Capital-surplus oil producers	25.8	8.0	51.1	63.0	23.2	29.0

Source: International Labour Organisation, World Labour Report, I
(Geneva, 1984).

Thus occurs the second phenomenon characteristic of domestic structural transformation in the developing world: the rapid transformation of the demographic structure, uniformly in favour of urban areas. The position of youth in this transformation was elaborated in chapter II, and the implications will be treated below. The general world-wide configuration can be seen in table 4 and figure I. In 1985, of the world's 35 largest urban agglomerations with populations of over 5 million, only 13 were in the developed world; in the year 2000, there will be only 10 in the developed world, and 25 in the developing world (table 14).

All this has major implications for the structure of employment in general, and for the employment of young people in particular. The breakdown of employment by sector is given in table 15. The share of the labour force in agriculture seems to have fallen between 1960 and 1980, on the average from 73 to 59 per cent, which is less than the fall in the share of agriculture in the GDP (table 13). The share of this labour force in industry appears to have risen, from 13 to 20 per cent, which is a little less than the increase of the share of industry in the GDP, from 30 to 39 per cent. The share of the service sector has gone up considerably: from 15 to 21 per cent for the labour force, and from 39 to 42 per cent for the GDP. When these trends are conflated with another indicator of domestic transformation - education, which was discussed above - the picture does not improve substantially. Changes in the education profile have tended to produce a better educated, and perhaps more personally independent labour force, often with high aspirations. They have also frequently resulted in the waste of educated people through unemployment, and their use in jobs for which their education would hardly seem relevant. The emphasis given to secondary and higher education has often implied an increasing educational gap between the young rural worker, who has probably never completed primary education (in any case of low quality), and the more privileged modern-sector workers.

Urban populations, 1950-2025

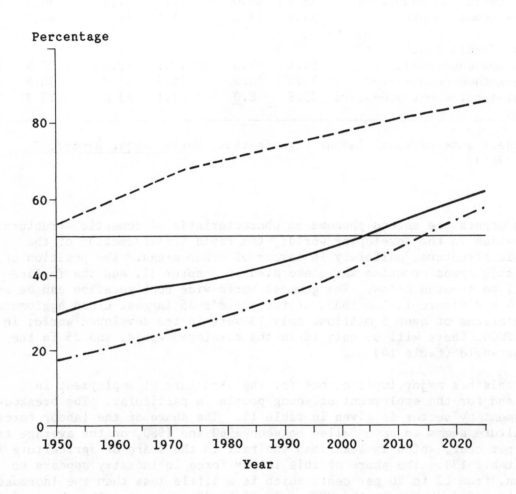

Percentage

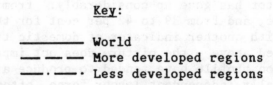

Key:

—————— World

– – – – More developed regions

–·–·– Less developed regions

<u>Source</u>: <u>Estimates and Projections of Urban, Rural City Populations,
1950-2025: The 1982 Assessment (ST/ESA/SER.R/58)</u>.

Table 14. World's largest agglomerations, 1985 and 2000

1985 Agglomeration/country/area	Population	2000 Agglomeration/country/area	Population
Mexico City, Mexico	18.1	Mexico City, Mexico	26.3
Tokyo/Yokohama, Japan	17.2	Sao Paulo, Brazil	24.0
Sao Paulo, Brazil	15.9	Tokyo/Yokohama, Japan	17.1
New York/North-Eastern United States	15.3	Calcutta, India	16.6
Shanghai, China	11.8	Greater Bombay, India	16.0
Calcutta, India	11.0	New York/North-Eastern United States	15.5
Greater Buenos Aires, Argentina	10.9	Seoul, Republic of Korea	13.5
Rio de Janeiro, Brazil	10.4	Shanghai, China	13.5
Seoul, Republic of Korea	10.2	Rio de Janeiro, Brazil	13.3
Greater Bombay, India	10.1	Delhi, India	13.3
Los Angeles/Long Beach, United States	10.0	Greater Buenos Aires, Argentina	13.2
London, United Kingdom	9.8	Cairo/Giza/Imbaba, Egypt	13.2
Beijing (Peking), China	9.2	Jakarta, Indonesia	12.8
Rhein-Ruhr, Federal Republic of Germany	9.2	Baghdad, Iraq	12.8
Paris, France	8.9	Teheran, Iran (Islamic Republic of)	12.7
Moscow, USSR	8.7	Karachi, Pakistan	12.2
Cairo/Giza/Imbaba, Egypt	8.5	Istanbul, Turkey	11.9
Osaka/Kobe, Japan	8.0	Los Angeles/Long Beach, United States	11.2
Jakarta, Indonesia	7.9	Dacca, Bangladesh	11.2
Tainjin, China	7.8	Manila, Philippines	11.1
Delhi, India	7.4	Beijing (Peking), China	10.8
Baghdad, Iraq	7.2	Moscow, USSR	10.1
Teheran, Iran (Islamic Republic of)	7.2	Bangkok/Thonburi, Thailand	9.5
Manila, Philippines	7.0	Tianjin, China	9.2
Milan, Italy	7.0	Paris, France	9.2
Chicago/North-Western Indiana, United States	6.8	Lima-Callo, Peru	9.1
Istanbul, Turkey	6.8	London, United Kingdom	9.1
Karachi, Pakistan	5.7	Kinshasa, Zaire	8.9
Lima-Callo, Peru	5.5	Rhein-Ruhr, Federal Republic of Germany	8.6
Bangkok/Thonburi, Thailand	5.2	Lagos, Nigeria	8.3
Madras, India	5.1	Madras, India	8.2
Hong Kong	5.1	Bangalore, India	8.0
Madrid, Spain	5.1	Osaka/Kobe, Japan	7.7
Leningrad, USSR	4.9	Milan, Italy	7.5
Dacca, Bangladesh		Chicago/North-Western Indiana, United States	7.2

Source: Estimates and Projections of Urban, Rural and City Populations, 1950-2025: The 1982 Assessment (ST/ESA/SER.R/58).

Table 15. Labour force structure: developing countries, 1960–1980
(Percentages)

Country/group	Agriculture		Industry		Services	
	1960	1980	1960	1980	1960	1980
All developing countries	72.6	59.1	12.8	19.9	14.5	21.0
Latin America and Caribbean						
Low-income countries	63.5	49.3	14.8	19.8	21.7	30.9
Middle-income countries	45.6	31.8	20.7	25.8	33.6	42.4
China	74.8	60.0	15.4	25.8	9.8	14.2
India	74.0	62.2	11.3	17.2	14.7	20.6
Asia						
Other low-income countries	76.4	65.5	8.1	11.8	15.5	22.7
Middle-income countries	68.0	52.5	12.2	19.4	19.8	28.1
Africa and Middle East						
Low-income countries	87.6	80.0	5.1	8.6	7.3	11.4
Middle-income countries	69.8	55.6	12.2	19.0	18.0	25.4
Capital-surplus oil producers	68.8	51.8	11.2	18.3	20.0	29.9

Source: International Labour Organisation, World Labour Report, I (Geneva, 1984).

This, however, is not always the case. Surveys conducted in several Latin American and Caribbean countries, and in Tunisia and India, show that young people flocking to the towns find work more easily than the town dwellers themselves, probably because they are less demanding. 44/ But the increase in the number of jobs in Government, industry and the modern sector in general is far from adequate to absorb the new additions to the urban labour force. Many young people thus resort to jobs in the informal sector, creating their own employment in such activities as trade and services, which require relatively little capital, but often entail marginalization. Many others who lack the necessary education, training or capital have no choice but to accept employment with wages below the legal minimum, job insecurity, and no social security. Apprenticeship in the informal sector, though it does provide a frequent source of training for young people, is a well known means of exploitation, which in turn prevents many of them from using this training for setting up their own ventures.

The general picture in the developing world, then, is one of extensive youth unemployment, even more extensive underemployment, and associated poverty. This is combined with a disjunction between the expectations of young people and the employment opportunities they are offered, whether they come from rural backgrounds or whether they are urban residents who have received a formal education. Any policy aimed at resolving the problem must therefore take into account both its qualitative and its quantitative dimensions. There have been many such policies, several of them successful. But all efforts continue to be hamstrung by the general economic situation in the world and its baneful reflections in particular developing countries.

Delinquency, crime and drug abuse

Passages from agrarian to predominantly industrial societies are, at best, perilous. What suffers the most in this process of change is traditional culture, especially traditional forms of social solidarity. While modern societies have their own forms of culture and solidarity, they are manifestly different from those of traditional society. The crucial issue here is the process of transition from one to the other. In situations of rapid urbanization, as is currently the case virtually all over the developing world, the transition process often does not keep pace with the rate of urbanization. These short-circuits in the process create something of a no-man's land between traditional and modern social formations. 45/ Relations between the generations are particularly vulnerable here. Traditional cultures sometimes lose their legitimacy in the eyes of young people - often a result of their being increasingly exposed to the ostensibly modern stereotypes of the mass media. These latter phenomena, taken by themselves, seldom constitute a coherent frame of reference. Many young people, in attempting to cross the boundary between the two areas of the social space, are thus drawn, willy nilly, into the no-man's land between them. The realities of economic crisis and recession further exacerbate this process, because they fragment various forms of social association. New forms are sometimes created. But they are often within the no-man's land. If not, they tend to be smaller and smaller groups which close their ranks. This, though an understandable form of social defence, is detrimental to social cohesion.

One defining characteristic of the no-man's land sketched above is an increasingly articulated machinery of crime and deviance. Many young people have no option but to join it. Others do so wilfully - often the result of romanticized stereotypes that are increasingly displayed in the mass media. In any event, whatever may be the drives and motivations, the consequence is various forms of juvenile delinquency, crime, and drug abuse. All this should be seen in the context of the general cultural crisis that so many young people face in the 1980s. From the point of view of ameliorating this situation, what is needed is more effort directed at providing young people with coherent forms of social participation - forms that are more constructive, and oriented towards generating integrated development.

Preventive devices must be balanced with curative ones, since the malady already exists in many parts of the world. Law enforcement, then, is not nearly enough; there is a need for the development of juvenile justice. If parental authority and other traditional forms of social control have tended to decline, young people clearly need another benign form of control before they have to face the harsh realities of the law enforcement apparatus. This could be provided by a comprehensive system of juvenile justice. Subsumed within this system would be, among other things, a whole variety of remedial methods for dealing with drug abuse, delinquency and petty crime. There is, of course, a well known need for more research into, and understanding of, this whole social area. But it is equally important for operational projects to keep pace with the development of theory and understanding.

Juvenile crime and delinquency continue to be serious problems all over the world. 46/ Criminality among youth has to be considered in the context of the social, economic and cultural milieu of each country, and the present data are insufficient to draw a detailed global profile of young offenders, or to ascertain the magnitude of youth crime in relation to that of other age groups. In recent years, the accuracy of official data on recorded crime has been a subject of much research and discussion. Information is usually supplied only when it conforms to legal categories, and thus it is often difficult to assess the social context in which many crimes occur. Several surveys of "hidden crime", or of "victimization", show that only a small proportion of conduct that could have been labelled as juvenile crime is, in fact, reported to official agencies. Experts generally agree that the "dark figure" of crime is greater for youth than for older population groups. At the regional preparatory meetings for both the International Youth Year and the Seventh United Nations Congress on the Prevention of Crime and the Treatment of Offenders, Governments drew attention to the increase and gravity of youth crime and delinquency. 47/ In the last two decades, many countries have seen a general upward trend in the incidence of recorded conventional crime committed by youth - which is statistically the most criminally active portion of the population. 48/

The intensity and gravity of juvenile crime and delinquency naturally differ from one country and region to another. In the centrally planned economies, rates of youth crime are reported to have stabilized, or even decreased. 48/ In some countries of Europe, the proportion of crimes committed by young persons was reported to constitute only a negligible fraction of total criminality. 48/ On the other hand, many countries, from different regions, have seen increasingly serious manifestations of youth violence, drug abuse, drug trafficking, assault and robbery. The largest part of recorded youth criminality, however, still appears to consist of property crime. 48/

Although young males are more represented than young females in most officially recorded offences, there is a considerable "dark figure" for female criminality. Commensurate with the tendency of greater economic and social equality for females, there appears to be a negative trend of a larger proportion of young women being involved in crime, mainly in large urban concentrations. Although young females are predominantly involved in petty offences, there is evidence from some countries of greater female involvement in more serious offences, such as drug abuse, group or gang violence, theft and robbery. Problems of juvenile justice are frequently compounded in the case of young women. Many recent studies indicate that at practically every stage of decision-making, young females are subject to differential measures which frequently imply real discrimination. For instance, females are more likely than males to be brought within the purview of the criminal justice system for status offences. Despite current beliefs about preferential treatment for female offenders, in many countries phenomena like running away from home, "incorrigibility" and "uncontrollability" are treated as contraventions of expected behavioural roles, and punished quite harshly. Studies of male and female delinquency indicate that girls charged with non-criminal-status offences have been, and continue to be, significantly over-represented in court cases. 48/

There is evidence of an apparent worldwide increase in youth criminal violence, especially in marginal sectors of the urban environment. The prevalence of inter-personal violence, street robbery, "mugging", sex crimes, school violence and vandalism has been recorded in both developed and developing areas. 48/ However, a great deal of this violence occurs at the bottom of the socio-economic pyramid, which is very wide in the developing countries. Violent youth offenders frequently come from deprived urban areas. In many cases, they are "street children" who have been exposed to violence in their immediate environment, either as observers or as victims. And they are often drop-outs from school, family and work. Their basic education, when they do have it, is poor; their primary socialization from the family is all too often inadequate. This leads to alienation, from family, parents and other elders in the community. A lack of clear guidance and emotional support engenders a painful search for identity, and thus does violence frequently become part of expressions of protest, or even of ideology.

There are, of course, a number of specific social and economic determinants of youth criminality, and squaring with these poses serious challenges to systems of education, social services and juvenile justice. 49/ Opportunity structures across the world are clearly the basic determinant, and, as indicated by the foregoing, far too many young people in many parts of the world have opportunities that can only be described as bleak. Destitution, bad living conditions, malnutrition, illiteracy, poor education, unemployment - all these make for the marginalization of young people, which, ipso facto, makes them vulnerable to exploitation as well as to involution in criminal and other deviant behaviour. Similar conditions, on a wider social level, work against a possible mitigation of this situation. Economic and social constraints, of one kind or another, are responsible for the inability of the family and the community to provide youth with an adequate support structure, and for the inability of institutions to provide adequate services and facilities.

The family is an irreplaceable environment for the harmonious development of the child, and when it faces crisis, or disintegrates, it cannot safeguard the wellbeing of the child. In the United States, for instance, more than one quarter of all families with children have only one parent. 50/ A majority of these are women; often they live below the poverty line. In 1983, one out of every three adults living below the poverty line in the United States was a woman. One elderly woman in six was poor. One poor family in every two was headed by a woman. 51/ Patterns such as this - the feminization of poverty - are replicated all over the world, and a growing number of poor, women-headed households is a characteristic common to many countries today. In situations such as these, as well as in a variety of other stressful situations, the family cannot provide an adequate supportive framework. Many young people thus grow up in the teeth of chronic instability and uncertainty. "Troubled families", for example, often create atmospheres of violence and conflict which do not conduce to a healthy upbringing. In many countries, there is increasing evidence of the abuse and exploitation of children by family members, or by those charged with their care. 52/ Though difficult to document, traumatic childhood experience has a well known pathology of crime and deviance. It is equally well known that the young are particularly vulnerable to victimization. There is much evidence from all over the world of child abuse, victimization and various forms of exploitation - like forced labour, prostitution and war - being key factors affecting youth crime and deviance. 52/

Drug abuse is an equally serious problem, and young people continue to be over-represented in the total number of drug addicts around the world. There appears to be an upward trend of youth involvement in drug offences, even in countries which have had relatively little experience of this phenomenon. 52/ Drug abuse by the young - especially hard drugs - is reported to be a growing problem in many countries, particularly in the larger cities. There has been an emergence of increasingly complex patterns of multiple drug abuse. These frequently involve combinations of a variety of narcotic drugs, psychotropic substances, alcohol, volatile solvents and substances not controlled under the international drug control treaties. On a regional basis, only parts of Eastern Europe, parts of Central Asia, including China, and a number of island States and territories in the South Pacific are relatively unaffected. 53/

This wide geographical spread of drug abuse, within and between countries, is accompanied by a range of consequences affecting young people in particular, and communities and societies in general. Among these are the general impairment of individuals' physical health, the spread of crime, including violent crime, prostitution and even homicide. Absenteeism from school or work has frequently been identified as a side-effect of drug abuse. The costs to society of maintaining treatment and other facilities, as well as those needed for guarding against crime generated by drug abusers, are not easy to quantify, but are doubtless considerable. Drug abuse, as it grows, tends to have a multiplier effect. Abusers, in order to finance their own habit, often have to commission crime, indulge in crime, or encourage others to abuse drugs.

In the course of its deliberations on youth crime, the Seventh United Nations Congress on the Prevention of Crime and the Treatment of Offenders (Milan, August-September 1985), pointed to the need for a sharper policy focus on youth drug abuse, drug trafficking and drug-related crime. The Congress, in an effort to reduce the need for the application of legal formalities and ensure justice for juveniles around the world, also called for the development of distinct measures for the prevention of youth crime. It was thus considered important to develop specific policy measures which would address the problems of specific categories of youth: those who are "endangered" or at "social risk", those who abuse and traffic in drugs, and young females, migrants and minorities. 54/

As increasing numbers of young people come into conflict with judicial systems, there is evidence of the adverse and often irreversible effects of legal interventions and sanctions in the early stage of human development. The United Nations Standard Minimum Rules for the Administrations of Juvenile Justice ("The Beijing Rules") adopted at the Congress, are an important advance in the field of juvenile justice. 55/ They are informed by a philosophy and procedure specifically applicable to young offenders. The Rules reflect the aims and spirit of juvenile justice, and are meant to serve as a model international instrument for the fair and humane treatment and handling of young persons in conflict with the law. 56/

Notes

1/ For a general discussion of marginality, see Peter Worsley, The Three Worlds: Culture and World Development (London, Weidenfield and Nicholson, 1984).

2/ Ruth Leger Sivard, Women: A World Survey (Washington, D.C., World Priorities, 1985), p. 5.

3/ Survey reported in Uno Mas Uno (Mexico City), 30 January 1978, cited in Worsley, op. cit.

4/ International Labour Organisation, World Labour Report, I (Geneva, 1984), p. 42.

5/ For a general discussion of participation, see Report on the World Social Situation, 1982 (United Nations publication, Sales No. E.82.IV.2), pp. 162-167.

6/ United Nations Educational, Scientific and Cultural Organization, Youth in the 1980s (Paris, 1981), p. 21.

7/ Ibid., p. 22.

8/ L. Rosenmayr and K. Allerbeck, "Youth and society", special issue of Current Sociology, vol. 27, No. 2/3 (1979), pp. 14-16.

9/ Report on the World Social Situation, 1982 ..., pp. 162-167.

10/ See P. Streeten and F. Stewart, New Strategies for Development: Poverty, Income Distribution and Growth, Oxford Economic Papers, vol. 28, 1976; M. S. Ahluwalia, "Inequality, poverty and development", Journal of Development Economics, No. 3, 1976, pp. 307-342; and Michael Lipton, Why Poor People Stay Poor: A Study of Urban Bias in the World (London, Temple Smith, 1977).

11/ See N. R. Sheth, The Social Framework of an Indian Factory (Manchester, 1968); Keith Hart, "Informal income and opportunities and the structure of employment in Ghana", Journal of Modern African Studies, No. 11, 1973; F. Lauda Jocano, Slums as a Way of Life: A Study of Coping Behaviour in an Urban Environment (Quezon City, University of Philippines Press, 1975); J. E. Perlman, The Myth of Marginality: Urban Poverty and Policies in Rio de Janeiro (University of California Press, 1976); and Larissa Lomnitz de Adler, Networks of Marginality: Life in a Mexican Shanty Town (New York, Academic Press, 1977).

12/ See E. O. Edwards, "Investment in education in developing nations: policy responses when private and social signals conflict", World Development, III, 1 January 1975, pp. 41-45.

13/ Statistics on education are drawn from United Nations Educational, Scientific and Cultural Organization, A Summary Statistical Review of Education in the World, 1960-1980 (ED/BIE/CONFINTED 39/Ref. 1, 12 July 1984).

14/ Ibid., section IX: Educational expenditure, pp. 68-71.

15/ Ibid., section III: Enrolment, pp. 15-42, for all data on enrolment.

16/ Ibid., section VI: Drop-out and repetition, pp. 55-59, for global figures.

17/ Ibid., section III.

18/ Ibid., section V: Teachers, pp. 43-54.

19/ Ibid., section VII: Foreign students, pp. 60-61.

20/ 1985 Report on the World Social Situation (United Nations publication, Sales No. E.85.IV.2), p.34.

21/ A Summary Statistical Review ..., section VIII: Illiteracy, pp. 62-67.

22/ These projections must be interpreted with caution; see the provisos in A Summary Statistical Review ..., p. 62.

23/ 1985 Report on the World Social Situation, ..., p. 32.

24/ Thorsten Husén, "Present trends in education", Prospects: Quarterly Review of Education, vol. 12, No. 1 (1982), pp. 45-56.

25/ Global statistics for the evolution of training may be found in United Nations Educational, Scientific and Cultural Organization, Technical and Vocational Education in the World, 1970-80: A Statistical Report (Paris, 1983).

26/ 1985 Report on the World Social Situation, ..., pp. 34-37.

27/ Ibid., p. 36.

28/ Ibid., p. 37.

29/ International Labour Conference, Report of the Director General (68th session, 1982) (Geneva, 1982), part I: What jobs for youth?, p. 10.

30/ Ibid., p. 15.

31/ By the International Young Christian Workers (YCW); cited in Report of the Director General (Geneva, International Labour Organisation, 1982), Part I: What jobs for youth?, p. 15.

32/ The studies cited in footnote 11, above.

33/ United Nations press release (ILO/2189), 16 November 1984.

34/ Report of the Director General ..., p. 18.

35/ World Labour Report ..., p. 3,335.

36/ Report of the Director General ..., pp. 18-19.

37/ World Labour Report ..., p. 43.

38/ Ibid., p. 46.

39/ Ibid., pp. 40-41.

40/ For a general discussion on employment in the centrally planned economies, see World Labour Report ..., pp. 75-97 and Report of the Director General ..., pp. 22-24. All data, unless otherwise indicated, are drawn from these two sources.

41/ 1985 Report on the World Social Situation, ..., pp. 71-73.

42/ Report of the Director General ..., p. 24.

43/ World Labour Report ..., p. 17. For a general discussion on the problem, see pp. 10-18.

44/ Report of the Director General ..., p. 25.

45/ For a general discussion, see Worsley, op. cit.

46/ "Youth, crime and justice", Report of the Interregional Preparatory Meeting for the Seventh United Nations Congress on the Prevention of Crime and the Treatment of Offenders, Beijing, 14-18 May 1984 (A/CONF.121/IPM/1, 27 June 1984).

47/ "The situation of youth in the Asian and Pacific Region" (SD/RPMIYY/1, 19 May 1983) paper presented to the Regional Preparatory Meeting for the International Youth Year, Bangkok, 26-30 July 1983; "The situation of youth in Europe" (IYY/ECE/RPM/2, 24 June 1983), paper presented to the Regional Preparatory Meeting on International Youth Year, Costinesti, 5-9 September 1983; "The situation and prospects of youth in Latin America" (E/CEPAL/CONF.75/L.2, 5 September 1983), paper presented to the Regional Preparatory Meeting on International Youth Year, San Jose, 3-7 October 1983; "The situation and needs of youth in Western Asia" (E/ECWA/SDP/W.G.I./3, 1 August 1983), paper presented to the Regional Preparatory Meeting on International Youth Year, Baghdad, 9-13 October 1983. International Youth Year: Regional Plans of Action, 1983 (United Nations publication, 1984); and reports of regional preparatory meetings for the Seventh United Nations Congress on the Prevention of Crime and the Treatment of Offenders: Europe (A/CONF.121/RPM/1, 29 July 1983); Asia and the Pacific (A/CONF.121/RPM/2, 29 July 1983); Latin America (A/CONF.121/RPM/3, 6 December 1983); Africa (A/CONF.121/RPM/4, 21 December 1983); and Western Asia (A/CONF.121/RPM/5, 17 January 1984).

48/ "Youth, crime and justice: working paper prepared by the Secretariat", (A/CONF.121/7, February 1985).

49/ "Report of the Secretary-General on relationships between crime and specific socio-economic issues" (E/AC.57/1984/5).

50/ United States Census Bureau estimates, reported in International Herald Tribune, 15 May 1985.

51/ Sivard, op. cit., p. 16.

52/ "Youth, crime and justice: working paper prepared by the Secretariat, "The situation of youth in the Asian and Pacific Region" (SD/RPMIYY/1, 19 May 1983), paper presented to the Regional Preparatory Meeting for the International Youth Year, Bangkok, 26-30 July 1983; "The situation of youth in Europe" (IYY/ECE/RPM/2, 24 June 1983), paper presented to the Regional Preparatory Meeting on International Youth Year, Costinesti, 5-9 September 1983; "The situation and prospects of youth in Latin America" (E/CEPAL/CONF.75/L.2, 5 September 1983), paper presented to the Regional Preparatory Meeting on International Youth Year, San Jose, 3-7 October 1983; "The situation and needs of youth in Western Asia" (E/ECWA/SDP/W.G.I./3, 1 August 1983), paper presented to the Regional Preparatory Meeting on International Youth Year, Baghdad, 9-13 October 1983. International Youth Year: Regional Plans of Action, 1983 (United Nations publication, 1984); and Reports of Regional Preparatory Meetings for the Seventh United Nations Congress on the Prevention of Crime and the Treatment of Offenders: Europe (A/CONF.121/RPM/1, 29 July 1983); Asia and the Pacific (A/CONF.121/RPM/2, 29 July 1983); Latin America (A/CONF.121/RPM/3, 6 December 1983); Africa (A/CONF.121/RPM/4, 21 December 1983); and Western Asia (A/CONF.121/RPM/5, 17 January 1984).

53/ "Situation and trends in drug abuse and illicit traffic: report of the Secretary-General" (E/CN.7/1985/2, 14 January 1985).

54/ Report of the Seventh United Nations Congress on the Prevention of Crime and the Treatment of Offenders, 26 August-6 September 1985 (A/CONF.121/22).

55/ The Beijing Rules were adopted by the Seventh United Nations Congress on the Prevention of Crime and the Treatment of Offenders. For the text of the Rules, see Report of the Seventh United Nations Congress .... See also "Draft standard minimum rules for the administration of juvenile justice: report of the Secretary-General" (A/CONF.121/14).

56/ The Rules contain specific principles governing the processing of young offenders at every stage, including institutional and non-institutional treatment. Among other things, emphasis is placed on: the proportionality of sanctions; the protection of rights; the preservation of well-being; fairness and equality; non-punitive intervention; diversion from the formal justice system; and the use of non-custodial and community-based sanctions as well as specialized services, personnel and programmes. The basic principles underlying the Rules are the following: (a) young persons in trouble with the law should be provided with carefully constructed legal protection; (b) pre-trial detention and institutionalization should be used as measures of last resort, unless there is no other appropriate response that will protect public safety; (c) institutionalized young persons should be kept in facilities separate from adults; and (d) the community of nations should do all it can, both individually and collectively, to provide the means for young persons to achieve a meaningful life.

V. REGIONAL PERSPECTIVES

The foregoing chapters have provided a general assessment of the global situation of youth in the 1980s. This chapter attempts to sharpen the focus, and conflate this general picture with specific perspectives from each of the five major regions of the world. Fundamental to the preparations for the International Youth Year, five regional preparatory meetings were held during 1983: at Addis Ababa in June, Bangkok in July, Costinesti in September, and San Jose and Baghdad in October. Each meeting had before it an assessment of the situation of youth in the particular region. On the basis of these assessments, the meetings elaborated five regional plans of action on youth. 1/ The regional perspectives outlined below try to follow the general positions adopted in the regional assessments, and attempt to build upon them by adducing further data where they appear germane.

Africa

Africa is the only major region of the world where the proportion of youth population in the year 2000 will be larger than it is in the present. In 1950, the youth population of Africa was 41.5 million. By 1985, it had more than doubled, to 105.4 million. In the year 2000, it is projected to increase to 170 million. As a percentage of total population, youth has constituted, throughout this period, 18-20 per cent. The most significant characteristic of African youth is its rural character: in 1984, some 65 per cent of the youth population was rural; by the year 2000, it will have decreased, but only to 53 per cent (see chapter II).

Rural youth thus constitutes the largest segment of the youth population of Africa. This group is confronted with four specific sets of problems: a general lack of basic social amenities in rural areas; a general problem of isolation, with very few organizations meant specifically for young people; a variety of contradictions between new aspirations and traditional values and systems; and limited access to land. 2/ These problems are subsumed within the larger issue of the food crisis in much of Africa. Agricultural performance continues to be an alarming problem: in 1985 the most severe drought in a decade reduced per capita food production for the fifth consecutive year. Although agricultural output in Africa is small in the total global context, it is the dominant economic activity in the region, often in the form of subsistence farming, for over 200 million people. 3/ When one considers this in light of the fact that 65 per cent of youth in Africa live in rural areas, the situation of youth begins to look extremely bleak, particularly since young people and children are often the worst affected by hunger and malnutrition. Moreover, the modest growth in Africa's agricultural production, with stagnation in food output, has wide repercussions on overall economic activitiy in the region. This, again, is especially relevant for the employment prospects of young people. In sub-Saharan Africa, 21 countries are currently in a critical situation with regard to food; 6 of them are threatened with widespread starvation. The aggregate food requirements of the 21 countries are estimated by the FAO to be 7 million tonnes, which is more than double that of the food aid received by these countries in 1983-1984. 4/ In 1984, the 21 produced 22.4 million tonnes of food, which was 12 per cent lower than the already drought-reduced output of 1983, and 21 per cent below the average of the previous five years. 5/

Much of Africa, then, appears to be at the wrong end of a paradoxical situation. In 1984, global staple-food production was nearly 10 per cent higher than in the previous year. While the industrialized nations struggle with food surpluses, Africa struggles with famine, because many low-income African countries, with inadequate foreign exchange reserves, have no access to the plentiful supplies of food on the world markets. Thus, in 1985, per capita staple food consumption levels are expected to decline in 19 of Africa's 37 low-income countries; in 24 of them, the level will be below that of 1969-1971. 5/ The problem, however, is not merely one of imbalances in the global economic system. While famines occur for a variety of reasons, the supply of food, population pressure, and income are not, in fact, the only variables to consider in the causation of famine. The availability of food is one thing; the entitlement to it is quite another. In this context, an entitlement is defined as: "... the set of commodity bundles that a person can command in a society using the totality of rights and opportunities that he or she faces". 6/ A famine can thus occur even in a good food-supply situation as a result of the collapse of the entitlements of particular social groups. 7/ A study of entitlement, then, must perforce go beyond purely economic considerations, and consider the political arrangements and distribution systems that affect people's actual ability to command commodities, the most basic of which is food. 8/ The four major sets of problems that young people in rural areas encounter - a general lack of social amenities; isolation; contradictory value systems; and limited access to land - should be seen in this general context.

The proportion of young people living in urban areas continues to rise steadily, a result of the fact that youth constitutes a majority in the large flow of migration from rural to urban areas. Public services have not been able to keep pace with these rapid rates of urbanization. While rural youth is a fairly homogeneous group, except for distinction of educational level, urban youth is far from being homogeneous, and many young migrants face a rapid process of marginalization. The ways in which this happens have been described above.

While there has been considerable educational progress in Africa, this applies essentially to enrolment in general education, and must be qualified by less apparent progress in vocational education, in reducing drop-out rates, and in educational coverage for young girls and women. 9/ In the decade of the 1970s, total enrolment in second level education grew at the rate of 13.9 per cent. Of this, general education constituted 14.5 per cent, teacher training 13.5 per cent, and vocational education only 6.7 per cent. In 1970, enrolment in vocational education represented 10.9 per cent of total enrolment in secondary education; in 1980 it had dropped to 5.7 per cent (see table 16). By way of comparison, figures for the rest of the world 10/ were 13.9 per cent in 1970 and 14.6 per cent in 1980. Within the African region, there was considerable variation in the proportion of second-level vocational education. In 1980, it varied from close to 1 per cent in countries such as Comoros, Niger and Zimbabwe, to over 20 per cent in countries such as Angola, Cameroon and Gambia. However, in the majority of African countries, the vocational training proportion represented less than 10 per cent of total secondary education.

Table 16. Distribution of second-level enrolment, by type of education, 1965, 1970, 1975 and 1980
(Percentage)

Region/country grouping	Total	Type of education		
		General	Teacher training	Vocational
World a/				
1965	100.0	84.3	1.9	13.8
1970	100.0	84.6	1.4	13.9
1975	100.0	84.7	1.3	14.0
1980	100.0	84.0	1.4	14.6

continued

Table 16 (<u>continued</u>)

Region/country grouping	Total	Type of education		
		General	Teacher training	Vocational

Developed countries b/

1965	100.0	81.8	1.2	17.1
1970	100.0	80.8	1.0	18.3
1975	100.0	80.5	0.7	18.8
1980	100.0	78.4	0.7	20.8

Developing countries c/

1965	100.0	87.9	2.9	9.2
1970	100.0	88.8	1.9	9.3
1975	100.0	88.7	1.8	9.5
1980	100.0	87.9	1.9	10.2

Africa

1965	100.0	80.1	6.0	14.0
1970	100.0	82.9	4.2	12.8
1975	100.0	86.2	4.3	9.5
1980	100.0	86.7	4.5	8.7

Africa (excluding Arab States)

1965	100.0	77.6	8.2	14.2
1970	100.0	82.9	6.2	10.9
1975	100.0	86.6	6.3	7.1
1980	100.0	88.1	6.1	5.7

Americas (Latin America and the Caribbean) d/

1965	100.0	67.4	8.9	23.7
1970	100.0	72.7	5.0	22.3
1975	100.0	72.0	4.5	23.5
1980	100.0	70.8	4.3	24.9

Asia c/

1965	100.0	90.6	0.8	8.6
1970	100.0	91.4	0.7	7.9
1975	100.0	91.5	0.6	7.9
1980	100.0	91.6	0.6	7.8

Asia (excluding Arab States) c/

1965	100.0	90.5	0.7	8.7
1970	100.0	91.3	0.6	8.0
1975	100.0	91.4	0.6	8.0
1980	100.0	91.5	0.6	7.9

Table 16 (continued)

Region/country grouping	Type of education			
	Total	General	Teacher training	Vocational

Arab States

1965	100.0	85.8	3.7	10.5
1970	100.0	86.8	2.1	11.1
1975	100.0	88.6	1.9	9.5
1980	100.0	87.6	1.9	10.5

Europe and USSR

1965	100.0	81.6	1.4	17.0
1970	100.0	80.8	1.1	18.1
1975	100.0	80.2	0.8	19.0
1980	100.0	77.1	0.8	22.0

Oceania e/

1965	100.0	86.2	5.2	10.3
1970	100.0	87.6	3.1	9.3
1975	100.0	85.7	2.7	12.2
1980	100.0	89.0	1.7	9.4

Source: United Nations Educational, Scientific and Cultural Organization, Technical and Vocational Education in the World, 1970-1980: A Statistical Report (Paris, 1983).

a/ Excluding Australia, China, Democratic People's Republic of Korea, New Zealand and North America.

b/ Excluding Australia, New Zealand and North America.

c/ Excluding China and Democratic People's Republic of Korea.

d/ Only data for Latin America and the Caribbean available.

e/ Excluding Australia and New Zealand.

Another matter of serious concern is the repetition and drop-out rate in primary education, particularly prior to the attainment of literacy. 11/ Thus, even if enrolment figures for primary education present an optimistic picture, high repetition and drop-out rates can, in fact, attenuate it. Figures available for 38 countries in Africa (including the Arab States), and covering some 60 per cent of total primary enrolment in the area, indicate the following weighted average survival rates for cohorts starting first-level education around 1980-1981: 83 per cent of the cohort is expected to reach the second grade, 80 per cent the third grade, and 71 per cent the fourth grade. The rates are higher in the French-speaking countries (84, 82 and 74 per cent), middling in the English-speaking countries (82, 77 and 72 per cent), and lowest in the Portuguese-speaking countries (57, 43 and 26 per cent). Repetition also poses something of a problem, particularly in the context of current doubts about how useful it actually is from the point of view of improving educational performance. The percentage of primary school enrolment constituted by repeaters for the whole of Africa (including the Arab States) shows a median value of 16 per cent. This subsumes considerable disparities, between, for instance, Sudan and Zimbabwe (0 per cent), on the one hand, and Chad and Sao Tome and Principe (37.6 and 46.6 per cent respectively), on the other.

Young women constitute a very sizeable proportion of the out-of-school young people in Africa. With few exceptions, school enrolment for girls is generally lower than that for boys. Traditional cultural influences relegate young women to a certain place in society, and many of them never even enter the world of formal education. Moreover, drop-out rates are higher among girls, and comparatively few girls are likely to attain higher academic levels. A number of African countries have made considerable efforts towards providing for the needs of young women through the provision of non-formal education and training programmes. However, given the formidable disadvantages that young women face in these areas, the quality of such programmes needs to be improved.

There are over 5 million refugees in Africa. This figure accounts for more than half of the total estimated global refugee population of about 10 million. Women and young people represent the majority of these homeless people. When the Second International Conference on Assistance to Refugees in Africa was convened in July 1984, among the countries requesting assistance were Somalia and Sudan, with approximately 700,000 refugees each; Burundi and Zaire, with 250,000 to 300,000; the United Republic of Tanzania with 180,000; and Angola and Zambia with 100,000 refugees each. A small country like Swaziland had 7,000 refugees for a population of half a million. 12/ A survey of one of the four principal settlements of Zimbabwe refugees in Mozambique in 1982 showed that only 500 of 5,000 refugees were adults. Another survey of refugees, in Kenya, showed that 20 per cent were 6 to 17 years old, and 43 per cent were 18 to 30 years old. 13/ Most countries, with the assistance of the international community, have tried hard to help young refugees, chiefly in the area of education and training. However, the problem grows progressively larger, and in some regions, such as southern Africa, the flow of refugees continues to swell.

Western Asia

In 1980, the youth population of Western Asia was 17.3 million, which constituted 20 per cent of the total population of the region. Of the youth population, 53 per cent was male. Some 55 per cent was adolescent, and the remaining 45 per cent young adults. This fact has many obvious implications for the planning process, particularly with regard to education. With regard to young people involved in the world of work, 27 per cent of the total youth population of the region was economically active. Of this, only 28 per cent were young women. Here again, along with education, is another major problem of the region: the need to integrate young women into society in general, and into the labour force in particular. 14/

The broad contours of the Western Asia region are formed by the region's rapid population growth, the young age structure of the population, large migrations, and a relatively low population density. The situation of young people here needs to be looked at in relation to this as well as in the context of the enormous transformation and upheaval which has characterized the region in the last few decades. While large transformations have been a global characteristic of this period, the Western Asia region has been affected by two unique sets of events, both of which have put a significant imprimatur on the population generally, and on youth in particular. These are the successive wars that have rocked the region, and the oil crisis. Wars always tend to decimate the youth population of the areas concerned. Much historical evidence can be adduced to substantiate this, and the experience of the Western Asia region has been no different: the petroleum factor has completely transformed the social and economic structure of the region, and has been responsible for changes as diverse as the inflow of huge masses of foreign labour and the creation of several detrimental consumer patterns among young people.

The Economic and Social Commission for Western Asia (ESCWA) region comprises some of the most open economies among the developing countries. 15/ Consequently, these economies have been particularly vulnerable to adverse external factors. During the 1980-1983 period, the region experienced a negative growth rate of 6.4 per cent (at constant 1980 prices). This is in marked contrast to growth rates achieved during the 1970s. GDP growth rates, however, varied considerably among various sub-groups of countries in the region. The figures for 1980-1983, at constant 1980 prices, were: -4.6 per cent for the Gulf Cooperation Council countries; 16/ -12.3 per cent for the diversified economies; 17/ and 4.8 per cent for the least developed countries. 18/ Despite efforts directed towards a more equitable distribution of income, disparities in income between and within the countries of the region are still very high. The region, after all, comprises countries with per capita incomes among the highest in the world as well as countries that belong to the least developed category.

Both the production and the export of oil in Western Asia have been hurt particularly severely by developments in the world economy. There has been a very substantial decline in the world demand for oil, a result, in the main, of the recession in the early 1980s, energy conservation in the industrialized countries, and a substantial increase in the use of other sources of energy. Oil consumption in the developed countries fell from 40.8 million barrels per day (mbd) in 1979 to only 34.5 mbd in 1982, and was estimated to be 33.8 mbd in 1983. There was a simultaneous increase in oil production by States non-members of the Organization of Petroleum Exporting Countries (OPEC) such as Mexico, Norway and the United Kingdom. Faced by the oil glut, the ESCWA countries cut their total oil production from approximately 19 mbd in 1979 to about 9.7 mbd in 1983, and the share of the region in world oil output declined from 30 per cent in 1979 to only 17.9 per cent in 1983. Thus, the combined oil exports of Saudi Arabia, Iraq, Kuwait, and the United Arab Emirates fell from 16.8 mbd in 1979 to 7.2 mbd in 1983.

The effects of the decline in oil revenues, and the concomitant slow-down in development efforts, have spread from the oil-exporting countries to the other countries of the region. Many of these latter are to some extent dependent for their development programmes upon financing from the oil-exporting countries. There are other linkages between oil and non-oil economies: a decline in the former spreads over into the latter, a result, inter alia, of a decline in the latter's exports, and in the remittances of its workers in oil-producing areas. Official development assistance from the oil-exporting countries of Western Asia declined significantly in the early 1980s: it fell from $9 billion in 1979 to $8 billion in 1981, and then again to $6.5 billion in 1982. Social development initiatives have suffered as a consequence.

Education is an area of considerable concern for the whole region. Indeed, one major pillar of the development strategy for the region is

manpower development through education and training. However, while there is
a surplus of young people educated in the fields of the humanities and the
behavioural sciences, there is a serious paucity of youth with technical
education. Stated another way, this is a regional manifestation of the
general global problem of the wide gap between formal schooling and the world
of work.

It is estimated that 75 per cent of the total youth population of Western
Asia still has virtually no access to formal education. 19/ Youth programmes
and services provided by Governments usually operate through formal education
institutions. This means that 75 per cent of young people cannot be reached,
and hardly feel the impact of these initiatives. Much more effort is needed,
therefore, to integrate out-of-school and marginalized young people. In 1980,
the total number of young people enrolled in educational institutions in the
region amounted to 3,431,759. This constituted about 20 per cent of the total
youth population. Though the ratio of female to male students has been
increasing, there is still a need for further improvement. Of the total
enrolment, female students comprised only 36 per cent. 19/ The early 1980s
saw a continuous expansion at all levels of education: primary, intermediate,
secondary and higher. However, in most countries there was a relative decline
in the average education growth rate in comparison with the rapid expansion of
education during the 1970s. 20/

Open unemployment is relatively low in the region; however, underemployment
is a general phenomenon, both in traditional economic activities as well as in
the modern sector. As noted above, in 1980, only 27 per cent of young people
in the region were economically active. This average balances much higher
percentages in the Gulf States with lower ones in the other countries. 21/
The employment situation in the region is closely linked to the distribution
of manpower. The migration of labour (of which young people often constitute
the majority) from rural to urban areas, and from labour-surplus to labour-
deficit countries, has created problems for both the supplying and the
receiving areas: shortages of skilled manpower in the former; difficulties of
effective integration in the latter. The size of the migrant labour force in
the countries of the Gulf Cooperation Council was 1.086 million in 1975, and
rose to 2.935 million in 1980. This shows an average annual growth rate of
20 per cent. In the labour-exporting countries, the proportion of labour that
migrated reached 5 per cent in 1979, varying from 2 per cent in Tunisia to
40 per cent in Jordan. World Bank projections indicated that this proportion
of migrant labour would rise to 8 per cent by 1985, varying from 38 per cent
in Jordan to 5 per cent in Egypt. 22/

These problems are, in some cases, exacerbated by immigrant labour coming
in from outside the region. In the countries of the Gulf Cooperation Council,
the national component of the total labour force averaged 42 per cent in 1980,
with the lowest level in the United Arab Emirates (10 per cent) and the
highest level in Oman (61 per cent). These figures should be seen in
conjunction with those for the total immigrant and total youth populations in
the same countries. In the Gulf Cooperation Council countries, then, the
foreign component accounts for 32 per cent of the total population. The
foreign youth population in these countries is 35 per cent of the total youth
population. 23/ In Kuwait, for instance, the immigrant population has
outnumbered indigenous Kuwaitis since 1961. Furthermore, the age and sex
structure of immigrant populations tends to be distorted because, being
immigrant labour, a disproportionate number are young and male. Much of this
immigration is a relatively recent phenomenon, and the long-run social
implications of it are still not entirely clear. Of specific interest
vis-à-vis the situation of youth, is the question of the availability of

programmes and services needed to facilitate the process of young immigrants' adjustment to the different kinds of societies they have encountered.

Young women, as in so many other parts of the world, are a particularly vulnerable sub-group of youth in the region. They constitute 47 per cent of the total youth population. Traditional cultural influences relegate them to a certain place in society, and many of them never even enter the world of formal education. Illiteracy among them thus remains a major problem. Girls' enrolment rates are lower than those of boys'. Girls' drop-out rates are higher. Young women's participation in technical education programmes is minimal, or even completely absent in some areas. In the labour market, young women hardly figure at all. When they do, their labour is not recorded statistically. This is especially so in the agricultural sector, and also, to a certain extent, in the personal service sector.

Another sub-group of youth that is virtually on the periphery of society is nomadic young people. That the sub-group is a sizeable one is clearly demonstrated by the fact that nearly 20 per cent of the total population of some States in the region is nomadic. 24/ Nomadic communities are characterized by spatial instability and the diverse kinds of isolation which this engenders. To plan for youth here is difficult, because the spatial unity and temporal continuity of the relevant plans and programmes are frequently tenuous.

The Arab world continues to suffer from endemic political instability. That this is the burden of the recent history of the region is clearly demonstrable. However, while an adequate appreciation of this must inform any understanding of the region, there is still a need to document the linkages between the political and historical milieu, on the one hand, and specific social groups, on the other. Youth constitutes one such group. Its involvement in the recent historical processes of the region has been manifest, e.g. in wars, political mass mobilization, anti-colonial or popular movements of one kind or another, and, increasingly, in articulated forms of student politics. However, the only way to go beyond general formulations like this is to examine the effects of the political milieu upon the situations of specific sub-groups of young people.

Palestinian youth constitutes one such sub-group. To analyse its situation is particularly difficult, because the normal parameters within which such analyses are located - the nation State - do not exist in its case. Concerted attempts have gone a long way towards remedying this situation. Estimates made in 1970 indicate that Palestinian youth accounted for 553,000 (18 per cent) of the total Palestinian population of 3,060,000. On the basis of these estimates, projections for 1980 put the total population at 4 million, and the youth component of it at nearly 800,000. 25/ One of the major problems involved in the process of implementing youth development plans for young Palestinians is the spatial problem of their dispersion in different geographical areas. Within the United Nations, the agency responsible for co-ordinating Palestinian refugee relief is the United Nations Relief and Works Agency for Palestine Refugees in the Near East (UNRWA). In 1984, 2,034,314 Palestinian refugees were registered with UNRWA. Of this total, 35 per cent lived in camps. The geographical distribution of these refugees, covering both those in camps and otherwise, was 38 per cent in Jordan (781,564), 20 per cent in the Gaza Strip (410,745), 17 per cent on the West Bank (350,779), 13 per cent in Lebanon (256,207), and 12 per cent in the Syrian Arab Republic (235,019). As regards the youth component of the refugees, 12 per cent were 15-19 and 10.3 per cent were 20-24 years old. 26/ These two groups together constituted over 22 per cent of the total, and, being youth, were, ipso facto, the most dynamic element among the refugees.

The situation of young people in Lebanon has worsened since the outbreak
of the Lebanese civil war in 1975. It was estimated, in 1980, that youth in
Lebanon numbered some 450,000. 27/ However, the figures will doubtless be
different now, on account of the number of young people migrating, as well as
the number of them who have been casualties in the war itself. The social and
psychological ramifications of war are well known. Equally well known is the
fact that these ramifications multiply in their effect upon young people.
Lebanese youth is thus in severe need of special programmes designed to heal
the wounds of war.

Asia and the Pacific 28/

In the region of the Economic and Social Commission for Asia and the
Pacific (ESCAP), the youth population is 263.4 million in East Asia and
319.3 million in South Asia. These figures constitute 20 per cent of the
total population of each of these areas. The rural/urban distribution of the
youth populations is 65 and 35 per cent for East Asia, and 70 and 30 per cent
for South Asia. Projections of this distribution for the year 2000 are 54 and
46 per cent (East Asia) and 59 and 41 per cent (South Asia) (tables 1 and 4).

For most of the ESCAP countries, the percentage of youth population is
around 18 to 20 per cent, or approximately one fifth of each country's total
population. This is even more significant when account is taken of those
below 15 years of age, many of whom will be entering the phase of youth in the
near future. Youth, therefore, represents a substantial portion of the
region's population and of the labour force of individual countries. This is
particularly significant, since the percentage of economically active young
people in relation to total youth population ranges, in individual countries,
from about 33 to 76.5 per cent.

A major constraint upon the capacity of many developing countries in the
region to improve the quality of life has been their failure to raise per
capita availability of goods and services. This can be attributed, in the
main, to continued population growth, often at very rapid rates. In virtually
all the region's developing countries, gross output has continued to increase.
So, unfortunately, has population, which absorbs a substantial part of the
gains. The consequence has been little improvement in per capita real income.
The problem is compounded by inequalities in the distribution of income, and
disparities in relative growth rates of population and income in different
sectors. This means that even when average per capita income has grown, the
real income of those concentrated in slow-growth sectors like agriculture,
where population growth is often the most rapid, has frequently stagnated or
even declined.

Thus, in the rural areas of many Asia and Pacific countries, young people
are among the most disadvantaged groups. Their problems are specific
manifestations of a general milieu characterized by poverty, exploitation,
lack of access to land, lack of stable work, illiteracy, and minimal
participation. Rural workers - many of them young - are seriously
underemployed, working short days or short seasons for very low wages. The
problem of underemployment, traditionally linked to the phenomenon of seasonal
labour, is now further complicated with the phenomena of cash-cropping and
mechanization.

Rapid population growth has had other negative effects on social
development. In those economies that have not been growing fast enough to
absorb an expanding labour force, the problems of unemployment have
intensified. This has also been the case in economies where the structure of

production has tended to emphasize capital-intensive rather than labour-intensive processes. In some rural areas of the region, the relationship between the so-called "green revolution" and employment is increasingly questioned. The technology that made the green revolution - a package of inputs such as improved seed, water, fertilizer, and also known as high-yielding variety (HYV) technology - was heralded, in the 1970s, as a path-breaking approach to the acceleration of agricultural growth and employment. Rapidly accumulating empirical evidence establishes the former, but questions the ability of HYV technology to improve rural employment, since it appears to favour mechanization. 29/ The majority of young people in the region are rural, and have not always derived much benefit from these changes.

Unemployment and underemployment among youth are serious problems in both rural as well as urban areas. Projections for the period from 1980 to the end of the century indicate that the rate of growth of the labour force will exceed the rate of population growth in at least 13 ESCAP developing countries. In the 1960s, there was only one such country in the region. In the 1970s, there were only 5. 30/ In the present decade, the number of persons of working age (15 to 64) in the region rose from 1.1 billion to 1.5 billion and is expected to reach 1.9 billion by the end of the 1980s. 31/ A major contributory factor is the change in the age structure of the population because of a decline in mortality rates. Thus, the youth population grows at a faster rate than the population as a whole. These increasing numbers of young people have to be provided with gainful employment, and this becomes progressively difficult. Youth unemployment, as a proportion of total unemployment, was, for instance, 55 per cent in the Philippines (1978), 60 per cent in Thailand (1982), 63 per cent in India (1981), 48 per cent in the Republic of Korea (1982), 49 per cent in Hong Kong (1982), and 58 per cent in Singapore (1982). 32/ Young women face an even more difficult employment situation. In the same countries and areas, the percentage of female youth unemployment was everywhere higher, except in the Philippines: 63 per cent in Thailand; 64 per cent in India; 79 per cent in the Republic of Korea; 62 per cent in Hong Kong; and 69 per cent in Singapore. 32/

The participation rates of young women in the labour force are generally lower than those of young men (see table 17). There are, however, consider-able disparities between different countries and areas. The female youth participation rate was very low in Afghanistan (9.3 per cent), Bangladesh (3.9 per cent) and Pakistan (6 per cent), but high in Indonesia (33.5 per cent) and Malaysia (44.7 per cent). It was even higher in Hong Kong (60.6 per cent), Singapore (63.5 per cent) and Thailand (74.2 per cent). This should be balanced, however, with higher unemployment rates among young women, as shown above.

Spatial shifts in the location of population, from rural to urban areas, are important determinants of the situation of youth. As noted above, a majority of the population in developing areas of the region is rural. However, in most of the countries, urban population growth rates have exceeded rural rates of growth in the last three decades (see tables 5 and 18). This is largely the result of rural-urban migration, of which young people are often the majority. The region's total rural population is expected to increase by only 21 per cent between 1980 and 2000. The total urban population, on the other hand, increased from 24 per cent a decade ago to about 28 per cent in the early 1980s. By the end of the century, the total urban population of the region is projected to be 1,380 million, which is double what it was in 1980. 33/ The problem of urban growth is exacerbated by serious imbalances in the distribution of population in urban areas. The condition of "primacy", where the largest city is at least twice the size of

Table 17. Economically active youth in selected developing ESCAP economies

Country or area	Year a/	Male youth			Female youth			Total youth			
		Total (thousands)	Economically active (thousands)	Participation rate (per cent)	Total (thousands)	Economically active (thousands)	Participation rate (per cent)	Total (thousands)	Economically active (thousands)	Participation rate (per cent)	Economically active youth in total active population (per cent)
Afghanistan	1979	1 300.0	987.1	75.9	1 236.7	115.2	9.3	2 536.7	1 102.3	43.5	32.5
Bangladesh	1979	5 569.9	4 169.3	74.9	5 260.1	204.2	3.9	10 830.0	4 373.5	40.4	25.8
Hong Kong	1980	595.0	391.4	65.8	556.0	337.1	60.6	1 150.9	728.5	63.3	31.6
Indonesia	1977	11 111.0	7 183.1	64.6	11 551.4	3 870.2	33.5	22 662.3	11 053.2	48.8	24.2
Malaysia (Peninsular)	1977	1 222.5	856.2	70.0	1 194.9	534.7	44.7	2 417.4	1 390.9	57.5	35.7
Pakistan	1981	6 764.0	5 063.0	74.9	6 004.0	362.0	6.0	12 768.0	5 425.0	42.5	25.6
Singapore	1980	309.0	213.8	69.2	291.6	185.2	63.5	600.5	399.1	66.5	36.9
Thailand	1978	4 213.6	3 302.3	78.4	4 253.9	3 178.8	74.7	8 467.5	6 471.1	76.5	31.6

Source: Economic and Social Survey of Asia and the Pacific, 1982 (United Nations publication, Sales No. E.83.II.F.1).

a/ Latest year for which data were available.

the second largest one, exists, for example, in Bangladesh, Pakistan, Philippines, Republic of Korea and Thailand. Other countries, such as Indonesia, Malaysia and Sri Lanka, appear to be moving towards the same situation of primacy. The consequence of this is that the large city in question tends to demand a disproportionate share of resources for social and economic development. A large influx into the big cities exacerbates already manifest difficulties of squaring urban population growth with the expansion of employment, housing and other services. Thus do negative phenomena like squatter settlements, congestion, poverty and crime, multiply. Resources, already scanty, are then increasingly diverted to cope with the problems of urban development and renewal. The process of young people becoming marginalized, particularly in large urban concentrations, has been discussed above.

Table 18. ESCAP region: average annual growth rate of urban and rural population, by major subregion, 1970-2000
(Percentage)

Subregion	Population	1970-1980	1980-1990	1990-2000
South Asia	Urban	4.0	4.5	4.3
	Rural	2.1	1.8	1.0
East Asia				
China	Urban	3.3	3.3	3.3
	Rural	1.1	0.5	0.1
Japan	Urban	2.1	1.3	0.9
	Rural	-1.6	-1.7	-1.4
Other	Urban	4.3	3.3	2.4
	Rural	-0.3	-0.4	-0.3
South-east Asia	Urban	4.2	4.5	4.3
	Rural	2.3	1.9	1.1
Pacific	Urban	2.7	2.4	1.8
	Rural	-0.1	-0.2	-0.1

Source: Economic and Social Survey of Asia and the Pacific, 1982 (United Nations publication, Sales No. E.83.II.F.1).

Although considerable efforts have been invested in raising educational levels in the region, a large percentage of rural youth - young women in particular - never even enter the formal educational system, and have minimal contact with non-formal education programmes. In urban areas, the proportion of unemployed graduates with secondary and tertiary education has increased. This is despite the fact that school enrolment ratios in the region have doubled in the last two decades, and the literacy rate of youth is as high as 90 per cent in some countries. Even school drop-out rates are generally on the increase. This essentially reflects the fact that school systems often do not cater to children who are unprepared, in their homes, for even a basic education. These children from low-income sectors often have to cope with the additional burden of linguistic difficulties, and the primarily middle-class values reflected in urban schools - values that are frequently alien to them. School thus becomes an experience of failure and rejection. In 16 countries surveyed in the region, the weighted average survival rates for cohorts starting primary education around 1980-1981, were expected to be 87 per cent for the second grade, 80 per cent for the third grade, and 75 per cent for the fourth grade. The rates, however, are much higher in the three countries of Oceania (95, 95 and 93 per cent respectively). 34/ With regard to repeaters as a proportion of those enrolled in primary education, several developing countries in the region showed high percentages: Bangladesh (17.8), Afghanistan (14.8), Bhutan (12.9), Sri Lanka (10.2) and Thailand (10.2). 34/

Enrolment ratios for secondary education are substantially lower than those for primary education in most of the developing countries of the region. For tertiary education, they are even lower. Among the factors contributing to this are the high costs of higher education, which impose pressure on many young people to enter wage or casual employment. There is sometimes evidence of parental opposition to education, particularly in the case of young women. In many cases, secondary or tertiary educational institutions are simply not accessible to young people in rural areas, and rural poverty minimizes possibilities of a move to the city for education. Finally, there is the generally perceived malady of disjunctions between academic curricula and employment requirements. In view of these considerations, and the fact that higher education absorbs more resources per student than basic education and training, many Governments are faced with dilemmas of deciding where to allocate scanty resources.

The access of girls and young women to educational facilities presents a varied picture in the region. In primary education, enrolment ratios are similar for males and females in many countries. However, in some other countries, the ratio for female enrolment is much worse. In Afghanistan, 93 per cent of young girls never went to school in 1979/80. In Bhutan, also, only 7 per cent of young girls were enrolled. For Pakistan, total female enrolment was 31 per cent as against 81 per cent for males. For India and Bangladesh, though the enrolment ratios were higher, substantial differences in male and female ratios were nonetheless manifest. In secondary education, disparities between male and female enrolment, as well as between countries and areas, are greater. Female secondary enrolment in Afghanistan, for instance, was as low as 1.2 per cent in 1979/80. It varied between 8 and 20 per cent in Bangladesh, India, Indonesia, Nepal and Pakistan. In some other countries and areas, such as China, Fiji, Hong Kong, Malaysia, Philippines, Republic of Korea and Singapore, there were ratios of 50 per cent or more. In tertiary education, only a very small proportion of young women were enrolled. In Hong Kong, Mongolia, Republic of Korea and Singapore, the rates ranged from 6 to 8 per cent. They were much less in most other developing countries in the region. The Philippines was a major exception, with nearly 29 per cent of women aged 20-24 years enrolled in tertiary education as of 1979. 35/

Latin America and the Caribbean

In 1984, the total youth population of Latin America was 80.4 million, which constituted 20 per cent of the total population. In 1960, the youth population was 38.6 million (17.8 per cent of the total); by 1980, it had almost doubled, to 73.6 million (20.3 per cent of the total); in the year 2000, it is projected to increase to 104.8 million (19.1 per cent of the total). Rates of urbanization have been very rapid in the region, and this is

reflected in the regional location of young people. In 1970, 59.5 per cent of
youth lived in urban areas; in 1984, the figure had risen to 69.6 per cent.
This reflects a youth urbanization rate of 4 per cent, which is significantly
higher than the global rate of 3.1 per cent. Between 1984 and the end of the
decade, the global rate will decline to 2 per cent; the rate for Latin America
will also decline, but to a lesser extent, and will be 2.3 per cent. Thus, in
the year 2000, 77.2 per cent of young people in the region will be urban
residents (tables 4 and 5).

Young people form a large portion of the economically active population
of the region. In 1980, it was estimated that youth constituted one third of
the total labour force, and 48.2 per cent of the total youth population was
incorporated into it. In urban areas, young people constituted 58.6 per cent
of the total urban active population. As successive cohorts pass through the
age structure of the population, the youth component of the economically
active population is expected to decrease from one third in 1980 to 27.5 per
cent in the year 2000. Despite this, the absolute number of persons
incorporated into the labour market is expected to be 4.1 million a year from
1980 to 2000. 36/ The proportion of young women in this annual figure is
projected to increase; so, also, is the rate of urbanization. Thus, in the
year 2000, young people will constitute 70.6 per cent of the economically
active urban population (table 19).

The most significant phenomenon in the transformation of the Latin
American occupational structure in recent years has consequently been the
decrease - in both relative and absolute terms - of the number of persons in
the agricultural sector. This is particularly pronounced among young people,
who consitute a majority of the flow of migration from rural to urban areas.
Agricultural participation rates among young people appear to have declined
faster than those for older sections of the population. In Argentina and
Chile, for instance, the percentages of youth in agricultural activities in
1960 were 19.3 and 26.4 per cent respectively; by 1970, they had decreased to
13.2 and 22.8 per cent. A sharper decline was observed in Mexico, which had
larger percentages of youth in the agricultural sector: 53.6 per cent in 1960
had dropped to 35.1 per cent by 1970. Similar phenomena have been observed in
countries such as Colombia, Costa Rica and Panama. 36/ Though the numbers of
young people in rural areas are declining, their problems are still compelling
ones. The rural youth is often compelled to enter the working world
prematurely; his educational attainments are far lower than those of his urban
counterpart. In Panama and Chile, for instance, 44 and 53.7 per cent of urban
youth have 10 or more years of education, whereas the figures for rural youth
are only 17.1 and 17.6 respectively. 36/ Young people in rural areas are thus
incorporated into a type of agrarian employment which, because of their low
educational level, they are unable to leave. Marginality thus reproduces
itself.

The most commonly adopted route out of these circuits of marginality -
migration - is often an illusory one: marginality in the countryside is only
replaced by marginalization in the city that the young migrant enters. It is
well known that the expansion of employment has not kept pace with the rapid
rate of urbanization in the region. Young migrants from rural areas then,
less educated, less culturally and psychologically prepared for the urban
milieu, become unemployed or underemployed. Many also join the burgeoning
informal sector, where the exploitation of labour is well known. The circuits
of marginality in the city thus become as restrictive as the ones in the
countryside left behind. Not all young people, of course, are in such a
situation. But the very fact of it contributes to perpetuate a phenomenon
that is general in the region: an increasing segmentation in the forms of

Table 19. Latin America: economically active population between 10 and 24 years of age, according to urban-rural area (1970, 1980 and 2000)

Country	Thousands of persons						Percentage of active urban population		
	1970		1980		2000		1970	1980	2000
	Urban	Rural	Urban	Rural	Urban	Rural			
Group A a/									
Argentina	1 888.9	649.4	2 191.7	597.5	2 749.0	506.0	74.4	78.6	84.5
Costa Rica	70.1	123.8	124.3	155.6	194.2	125.0	36.2	44.4	60.8
Cuba	371.3	293.7	515.4	306.1	527.7	169.1	55.8	62.7	75.7
Chile	574.9	213.4	797.5	234.7	956.6	184.5	72.9	77.3	83.8
Uruguay	201.3	58.2	221.9	53.6	260.6	45.1	77.6	80.5	85.2
Group B b/									
Bolivia	170.6	271.3	251.7	295.0	494.9	431.4	38.6	46.0	53.4
Ecuador	213.6	377.8	342.9	459.6	793.8	597.5	36.1	42.7	57.1
El Salvador	170.5	280.8	272.1	351.1	594.4	472.1	37.8	43.7	55.7
Guatemala	199.3	409.9	298.1	530.7	582.3	784.6	32.7	36.0	42.6
Haiti	143.6	674.3	213.6	815.9	468.2	1 107.2	17.6	20.7	29.7
Honduras	84.4	208.5	152.6	262.9	446.3	327.6	28.8	36.7	57.7
Nicaragua	84.1	124.4	140.4	148.5	338.3	196.0	40.3	48.6	63.3
Paraguay	113.3	165.9	157.8	250.9	301.8	361.3	40.6	38.6	45.5
Peru	658.1	482.3	1 005.6	557.7	1 969.8	636.2	57.7	64.3	75.6
Dominican Republic	192.1	360.1	327.5	448.9	588.4	419.1	34.8	42.2	58.4
Group C c/									
Brazil	4 966.7	5 714.0	7 628.6	6 268.0	12 995.7	5 594.9	46.5	54.9	69.9
Colombia	1 377.5	968.2	2 078.8	1 062.5	3 041.0	857.5	58.7	66.2	78.0
Mexico	2 605.3	2 150.2	4 293.3	2 500.1	8 725.1	2 667.4	54.8	63.2	76.6
Panama	86.3	88.8	133.7	98.5	213.0	85.8	49.3	57.6	71.3
Venezuela d/	667.4	241.4	1 126.2	318.8	2 077.8	378.1	73.4	77.9	84.6
Latin America	14 839.3	13 856.4	22 273.7	15 716.6	38 318.9	15 946.4	51.7	58.6	70.6

Source: "Situation and prospects of youth in Latin America" (E/CEPAL/CONF.75/L.2, 5 September 1983).

a/ Countries of early urbanization, low fertility rate and high life expectancy.

b/ Countries of late urbanization, high fertility rate and low life expectancy.

c/ Countries of high polarization.

d/ Excluding active population between 10 and 14 years of age.

occupational integration of young people, and the consequent sharp polarization
between different social strata of youth.

Female labour is often not recorded statistically, especially in the
agricultural sector. Despite gaps in information, however, there is some
evidence of a growing incorporation of young women into the labour force.
The total economically active population of the region increased at a rate of
2.9 per cent between 1970 and 1980. The economically active female population
grew in the same period at a rate of 3.6 per cent. The highest participation
rates among women were recorded among young women in the 20-24 age group.
However, this tendency of increasing numbers of women in the labour force has
not always been a positive one, because of the quality of work involved. It
is estimated that in 1980 the informal sector absorbed 14 per cent of the
total economically active population of urban areas in Latin America.
Domestic service absorbed around 6 per cent, and a substantial proportion of
this was constituted by young women. Some figures for a major city in the
region were cited in chapter II. However, in some countries for which
information is available, there appears to be a decrease in the number of
young women performing domestic services. In Chile, 48.4 per cent of those in
the domestic service sector in 1960 were young women; by 1970 the figure had
dropped to 39.9 per cent, and by 1980 to 29.3 per cent. A similar trend was
recorded in Panama, where figures for the same years were 40, 36.3 and
28.1 per cent. 37/ These tendencies, however, do not in themselves mitigate
the general tendency of the polarization of youth described above, or the fact
that there are even stronger manifestations of it in the case of young women.

A lack of employment opportunities is probably the greatest problem
facing young people in the region. Open unemployment rates of 15 per cent
among urban populations are more than common. In many cases, young people,
particularly in the 20-24 age group, constitute half or more than half the
total number of unemployed persons. Thus, youth unemployment, as a percentage
of total employment, was 46 per cent in Argentina (1982), 62 per cent in the
Bahamas (1979), 56 per cent in Barbados (1982), 82 per cent in Colombia (1980),
76 per cent in Costa Rica (1982), 48 per cent in Chile (1981), 59 per cent in
Jamaica (1981), 56 per cent in Martinique (1980), 74 per cent in Panama (1979),
and 56 per cent in Venezuela (1982). 32/ These figures are for open employment.
The problem of underemployment is often even worse, and many young people in
such situations are in the informal sector, and marginalized. A survey of a
marginal area in one of the major cities of the region showed that 43 per cent
of employed persons in the 15-18 age group were either in casual jobs or in
jobs with fluctuating income; another 14 per cent worked as domestic servants
and 12 per cent in the Government Minimum Employment Plan. Only 25 per cent
had regular jobs with steady incomes, and half of these worked as messenger
boys or maintenance workers. 38/

In Latin America, particularly the urbanized parts of it, education seems
to become more and more a discriminatory variable. This points towards a
possible linkage between poverty and educational deficiency. While great
changes have taken place vis-à-vis education in the region, a lot of them have
been relatively recent, and their effect will be seen only in the future.
Though illiteracy has generally become residual among young people, countries
with large agricultural populations or with a substantial indigenous ethnic
component still record illiteracy figures of 15 per cent or more. Closely
connected to this is the fact that though nearly all children in the region
have access to primary school, only half of them manage to complete an average
educational cycle of six years. In 21 countries of the region, the weighted
average survival rates for children starting primary education around
1980-1981 are among the lowest in the world. Thus, 76 per cent of those

enrolled will survive to the second grade, 69 per cent to the third grade, and 63 per cent to the fourth grade. By contrast, comparable figures for 88 developing countries averaged 82, 76 and 69 per cent. 34/ The expansion of literacy is clearly qualified by phenomena such as these. Figures for rates of repetition in primary education in 1980-1981 underscore the point. Six countries (Argentina, Costa Rica, Cuba, El Salvador, Mexico and Venezuela) had repetition rates, i.e. the number of repeaters as a percentage of total enrolment, of between 5 and 9.9 per cent. In another six countries (Chile, Ecuador, Grenada, Panama, Paraguay and Uruguay) the rate was between 10 and 14.9 per cent. A further eight countries and areas had rates higher than 15 per cent: Nicaragua (15.3), St. Pierre Miguelon (15.8), Honduras (16.2), Guatemala (16.7), Haiti (17.8), Dominican Republic (18), Peru (18.5), and Brazil (20.4). 34/

Vocational education has made considerable progress in the region. 39/ In 14 countries and areas 40/ for which figures are available, vocational education accounted for 24 per cent of total secondary enrolment in 1970. Through the decade, it grew at a very high annual growth rate in comparison with general education - 6.6 per cent as against only 0.6 per cent. By 1980, vocational education accounted for approximately 35.5 per cent of total secondary enrolment, a fairly high proportion compared with the global average of 15 per cent.

Tables 20 and 21 show the distribution of enrolment by type of education in 1970 and 1980 in the region. 40/ Considerable variations are apparent, from a high in countries such as Argentina and Brazil, where vocational education accounts for 66 and 59 per cent of enrolment, respectively, to a low in Suriname, Paraguay and Venezuela with less than 5 per cent. The gap was not as great in 1970. Argentina already had the highest figure, with 58 per cent of enrolment in vocational education, followed by Chile with 33 per cent. As for the lowest figures, none of the countries showed less than 5 per cent and only three countries (Guyana, Paraguay and Suriname) less than 10 per cent. In addition to the increase in vocational education's share of enrolment in Argentina, it should also be noted that proportional enrolment in vocational education doubled in Brazil (from 29 to 59 per cent). The dramatic decrease in Venezuela (from 32 to 5 per cent) reflects the fact that, following the educational reform of 1975, vocational education and teacher training in the first stage of the secondary level are now considered to be part of general education.

The development described above is confirmed by the growth rates of general and of vocational education presented in table 22. In Argentina, vocational education grew at a rate of 4.6 per cent per annum, compared with 1 per cent for general education; in Brazil, at a rate of 24.7 per cent, as against 4.3 per cent for general education. The decline noted in Peru is due mainly to the different classification criteria adopted following a reform in the structure of education. The considerable growth of vocational education in Guyana and Suriname (10.3 per cent per year as against 3 per cent, and 15.9 per cent as against 4 per cent, respectively) should also be noted. The regression found in Venezuela can be explained by the above-mentioned reform of the educational system (with comparable figures, the growth rate would have been approximately 7 per cent).

Europe and North America

In 1984, the youth population of Europe numbered 76.8 million, which constituted 15 per cent of the total European population. The rural/urban distribution of this youth population was 27 per cent and 73 per cent

Table 20. Latin America: distribution of second-level enrolment,
by type of education, 1970
(Absolute figures and percentages)

Country	Total second-level (= 100 per cent)	Types of second-level education					
		General		Teacher-training		Vocational	
		Total	Percentage	Total	Percentage	Total	Percentage
Argentina	976 979	405 435	41.5	566	0.1	570 978	58.4
Bolivia a/	99 751	84 077	84.3	5 222	5.2	10 452	10.5
Brazil a/	1 119 421	549 343	49.1	248 798	22.2	321 280	28.7
Chile	302 064	202 506	67.0		-	99 558	33.0
Colombia	750 055	538 479	71.8	59 990	8.0	151 586	20.2
Ecuador b/	216 727	182 514	84.2	10 203	4.7	24 010	11.1
Guyana c/	60 412	57 093	94.5	259	0.4	3 060	5.1
Paraguay	55 777	48 742	87.4	3 545	6.4	3 490	6.2
Peru	546 183	453 001	82.9		-	93 182	17.1
Suriname	23 504	20 926	89.0	1 228	5.2	1 350	5.8
Uruguay	174 300	132 125	75.8	6 217	3.6	35 958	20.6
Venezuela	425 146	279 867	65.8	11 664	2.7	133 615	31.5

Source: United Nations Educational, Scientific and Cultural Organization, Technical and Vocational Education in the World, 1970-1980, A Statistical Report (Paris, 1983).

a/ Data refer to 1971.

b/ Data on general education include evening schools.

c/ Data on general education refer to public and aided schools only.

Table 21. Latin America: distribution of second-level enrolment,
by type of education, 1980
(Absolute figures and percentages)

Country	Year	Total second-level (= 100 per cent)	Types of second-level education					
			General		Teacher-training		Vocational	
			Total	Percentage	Total	Percentage	Total	Percentage
Argentina	1979	1 296 839	441 617	34.1	-	-	855 222	65.9
Brazil	1978	2 537 949	736 041	29.0	298 941	11.8	1 502 967	59.2
Chile	1980	538 309	369 180	68.6	-	-	169 129	31.4
Colombia	1980	1 891 530	...	...	...	...	397 820	...
Ecuador a/	1979	535 445	475 857	88.9	-	-	59 588	11.1
Guyana	1975	71 327	66 326	93.0	-	-	5 001	7.0
Paraguay	1978	101 126	96 559	95.5	-	-	4 567	4.5
Peru	1980	1 203 116	1 151 748	95.7	-	-	51 368	15.1
Suriname	1978	34 372	28 636	83.3	1 342	3.9	4 394	4.3
Uruguay	1978	180 678	130 504	72.2	4 511	2.5	45 663	25.3
Venezuela b/	1979	820 660	751 356	91.6	29 040	3.5	40 264	4.9

Source: United Nations Educational, Scientific and Cultural Organization, Technical and Vocational Education in the World, 1970-1980, A Statistical Report (Paris, 1983).

a/ Data on general education include evening schools.

b/ Following the 1975 reorganization of the educational system, data reported for general education include those for the first cycle of teacher-training and vocational education.

Table 22. Latin America: Enrolment in general secondary education
and in vocational education, 1970-1980
(Absolute figures and annual growth rates)

Country	General education			Vocational education		
	1970 a/	1980 a/	Annual growth percentage	1970 a/	1980 a/	Annual growth percentage
Argentina	405 435	441 617	1.0	570 978	855 222	4.6
Brazil b/	549 343	736 041	4.3	321 280	1 502 967	24.7
Chile	202 506	369 180	6.2	99 558	169 129	5.4
Colombia	538 479	1 187 148	12.0	151 586	348 590	12.6
Ecuador	182 514	475 857	11.2	24 010	59 588	10.6
Guyana c/	57 093	66 326	3.0	3 060	5 001	10.3
Paraguay	48 742	96 559	8.9	3 490	4 567	3.4
Peru	453 001	1 151 748	9.8	93 182	51 368	-5.8
Suriname	20 926	28 636	4.0	1 350	4 394	15.9
Uruguay	132 125	130 504	-0.2	35 958	45 663	3.0
Venezuela d/	279 867	751 356	11.6	133 615	40 264	-11.3

Source: United Nations Educational, Scientific and Cultural Organization, Technical and Vocational Education in the World, 1970-1980, A Statistical Report (Paris, 1983).

a/ Data refer to the years 1970 and 1980 or to the closest available years.

b/ Following the reorganization of the educational system in 1971, the duration of general education at the second level was reduced from 7 to 3 years.

c/ 1970 figures on general education refer to public and aided schools only.

d/ Following the reorganization of the educational system in 1975, data reported for general education incude those for the first cycle of teacher-training and of vocational education.

respectively, and is projected to be 21 and 73 per cent in the year 2000. The
North American youth population was 44.8 million, which constituted 17 per cent
of the total. The rural/urban distribution of this youth population was 20
and 80 per cent respectively, and is projected to be 16 and 84 per cent in the
year 2000 (tables 1 and 4).

The present generation is the most widely educated one in the history of
Europe and North America. Many young people have obtained a level of
education that is well beyond what was once considered average. There has
been a commensurate increase in opportunities for vocational and technical
training. In Europe and the USSR, technical and vocational education grew
from 1970 to 1980 at an annual rate of 3.6 per cent, which was much faster
than general secondary education, which grew at an annual rate of 1.2 per cent.
Between 1965 and 1970, vocational education grew at an annual rate of 4.5 per cent,
against 2.9 per cent for general education. The proportion of vocational
education in secondary education also rose, from 18 per cent in 1970 to 22 per cent
in 1980 41/ (see table 23). In the United States, the proportion of technical
and vocational education is fairly high, at 37 per cent. However, data for
the United States are often based on double counts, since the structure of
secondary education allows students to enroll in vocational education while
continuing to pursue regular courses in general education. This is also the
case in Canada. 42/ While there is much evidence, from all over Europe and
North America, of education in general becoming more responsive to concepts of
equality and the rights of all citizens to participate in the various decision-
making processes which concern them, 43/ there are still considerable
difficulties concerning the disjunction between formal schooling and work.
There is also the general problem, which concerns both education as well as
employment, of the under-utilization of human resources. These problems have
already been outlined in chapter IV, in the contexts of the market oriented as
well as the centrally planned economies.

In Western Europe and North America, the problem of youth unemployment
has been assuming increasingly serious proportions. Even in areas where youth
unemployment per se hardly exists, related questions have assumed significance:
underemployment, job satisfaction, working conditions, and the value of the
work performed. In recent years, the tendency of low economic growth has made
the prospects of improving youth employment look very dim. In the early
1980s, for instance, some countries had to face youth unemployment figures
that were as high as 40 to 50 per cent. Thus, youth unemployment, as a percentage
of total unemployment, was at the following levels in 1982: Italy, 62;
Portugal, 60; Turkey, 55; Spain, 54; Luxembourg, 47; Netherlands, 44; Canada, 43;
United States, 41; and Austria, 40. In Belgium and the United Kingdom, it was
at the borderline level of 39 per cent. 32/

The prospects of improvement in the near future do not look very bright.
Youth unemployment is, of course, a factor of general employment, and this,
according to a recent OECD forecast, will only show a slight improvement in
1986. 44/ In 12 OECD countries, 45/ 8 million young people were unemployed in
1980. This comprised 12.9 per cent of the total youth labour force (see table 24).
The following year, 1981, the figure had gone up to 9.1 million, which was
was 14.5 per cent of the youth labour force. 1982 saw a further increase, to
10.7 million, and 17.3 per cent. 1983 appears to have been the peak, with
10.9 million, and 17.7 per cent of the youth labour force being unemployed. A
very slight decline was observed in 1984, to 10.4 million and 16.8 per cent. 46/
Assessments of 1985 and forecasts for 1986, however, point to little change:
10.25 million and 16.75 per cent. This is because improvements in the United
States will be balanced by declines in some parts of Europe. 46/

Table 23. Europe, North America and USSR: distribution of second-level enrolment,
by type of education, 1980
(Absolute figures and percentages)

Country or area	Year	Total second-level (= 100 per cent) Total	Types of second-level education					
			General		Teacher-training		Vocational	
			Total	Percent-age	Total	Percent-age	Total	Percent-age
Albania	1980	163 866	30 780	18.8	604	0.4	132 482	80.0
Andorra	1975	1 753	1 753	100.0	–	–	–	–
Austria	1980	739 702	583 382	78.9	5 339	0.7	150 981	20.4
Belgium	1976	811 608	517 022	63.7	–	–	294 586	36.3
Bulgaria	1980	314 753	91 863	29.2	–	–	222 890	70.8
Canada a/	1976	2 840 284*	2 587 871	91.1	–	–	252 413*	8.9
Czechoslovakia	1980	388 561	145 395	37.4	14 457	3.7	228 709	58.9
Denmark b/	1980	498 944	372 948	74.7	–	–	125 996	25.3
Finland c/	1980	444 165	341 054	76.8	872	0.2	102 239	23.0
France	1980	5 015 447	3 911 054	78.0	–	–	1 104 393	22.0
German Democratic Republic	1980	506 412	46 927	9.3	–	–	459 485	90.7
Germany, Federal Republic of	1980	4 300 740	3 690 340	85.8	–	–	610 400	14.2
Gibraltar	1980	1 811	1 770	97.7	–	–	41	2.3
Greece d/	1979	725 263	618 688	85.3	–	–	106 575	14.7
Hungary	1980	202 788	89 400	44.1	5 897	2.9	107 491	53.0
Iceland	1980	26 643	19 091	71.7	168	0.6	7 384	27.7
Ireland	1980	300 601	286 619	95.3	–	–	13 982	4.7
Italy	1980	5 308 595	3 493 003	65.8	236 218	4.4	1 579 374	29.8
Luxembourg	1980	24 171	16 974	70.2	53	0.2	7 144	29.6
Malta	1980	25 501	21 377	83.8	–	–	4 124	16.2
Monaco e/	1980	2 065	1 314	63.6	–	–	751	36.4
Netherlands	1980	1 391 485	823 730	59.2	7 190	0.5	560 565	40.3
Norway	1980	360 776	279 266	77.4	345	0.1	81 165	22.5
Poland	1980	1 673 869	345 214	20.6	18 703	1.1	1 309 952	78.3
Portugal	1977	499 557	409 045	81.9	8 128	1.6	82 384	16.5

continued

Table 23 (continued)

Country or area	Year	Total second-level (= 100 per cent) Total	Types of second-level education					
			General		Teacher-training		Vocational	
			Total	Percentage	Total	Percentage	Total	Percentage
Romania	1980	871 257	80 879	9.3	6 317	0.7	784 061	90.0
San Marino	1980	1 219	1 219	100.0	-	-	-	-
Spain	1980	3 976 747	3 088 026	77.7	-	-	888 721	22.3
Sweden	1980	606 833	443 355	73.1	73	0.0	163 405	26.9
Switzerland	1980	459 590	425 203	92.5	10 128	2.2	24 259	5.3
United Kingdom	1980	5 341 849	5 087 036	95.2	-	-	254 813	4.8
United States	1978	29 478 370*	18 517 650	62.8	-	-	10 960 720*	37.2
Yugoslavia	1980	2 426 077	1 835 636	75.7	2 633	0.1	587 808	24.2
USSR	1980	20 274 500	17 355 900	85.6	160 200	0.8	2 758 400	13.6

Source: United Nations Educational, Scientific and Cultural Organization, Technical and Vocational Education in the World, 1970-1980, A Statistical Report (Paris, 1983).

a/ Data on vocational education represent full-time enrolment in Public Trade Schools, Comprehensive Schools (pre-employment and skill-upgrading) and Nursing Assistant Schools.

b/ Data on vocational education include full-time apprenticeship training.

c/ Data on general education include special education.

d/ Data on general education include evening schools.

e/ Data refer to public education only.

f/ Data on general education include special education; the figure on vocational education also includes students enrolled in general education.

Table 24. Youth unemployment in selected OECD countries a/

Country	1980	1981	1982	1983	1984	1985 h/	1986 h/
	Per cent of total youth labour force						
United States	13.3	14.3	17.0	16.4	13.3	12.5	12.5
Japan	3.6	4.0	4.4	4.5	4.9	4.7	5
Germany, Federal Republic of b/	3.9	6.5	9.6	10.8	10.1	9.2	9
France c/	15.0	17.0	20.2	21.1	26.1	29	31
United Kingdom d/	14.1	18.1	23.1	23.2	21.8	21.5	21
Italy	25.2	27.4	29.7	32.0	34.1	35.2	37
Canada	13.2	13.3	18.7	19.9	17.9	17.2	17
Total, seven countries	12.2	113.7	16.5	16.7	15.5	15.2	15.5
Australia e/	12.3	10.8	12.9	18.0	16.1	14.5	14
Finland	9.0	9.7	10.5	11.3	10.5	9.7	10.2
Norway	5.4	5.8	8.1	9.7	7.6	6.7	6.5
Spain f/	28.5	33.7	36.9	38.9	44.1	46	46
Sweden	5.1	6.3	7.6	8.0	6.0	5.5	6
Total, twelve countries g/	12.9	14.5	17.3	17.7	16.8	16.7	16.7
	Millions						
Seven countries	6.8	7.7	9.2	9.2	8.5	8.5	8.5
Twelve countries	8.0	9.1	10.7	10.9	10.4	10.2	10.2

Source: OECD Economic Outlook, 37 (Paris, 1985).

a/ The term "youth" generally refers to the 15-24 age group with a few exceptions: the age group is 14-24 in Italy and 16-24 in the United States, United Kingdom, Spain and Sweden. Data refer to the total youth labour force in all countries except Australia and Canada where the armed forces are excluded from the youth labour force. Data for Canada, Finland, Japan, Sweden and the United States are averages of monthly figures while data for Italy and Norway are averages of quarterly data.

b/ Unemployment figures refer to the registered unemployed at the end of September of each year. Labour force figures are annual averages based on various national sources, including the microcensus.

c/ Data refer to March of each year, except 1982 when the data refer to April-May. Conscripts are included in the labour force aged 15-24.

d/ Unemployment figues refer to claimants in July of each year, from 1982 onwards they include non-claimants in July of each year, from 1982 onwards they include non-claimant school leavers. Labour force data are estimated from several sources including the EEC Labour Force Sample Survey and refer to June of each year.

e/ Data refer to August of each year.

f/ Data refer to the last quarter of each year.

g/ These countries accounted for about 85 per cent of the youth labour force in the OECD area in 1979.

h/ Forecast.

Young women continue to face a difficult situation in some parts of Europe and North America. They still maintain narrow occupational aspirations, and have difficulty in entering occupations that have traditionally been held by men. Traditional attitudes, prejudice and discrimination have been the principal reasons for this. In spite of different programmes and schemes in many countries, young women are still a minority in skilled occupations - for example, the mechanical and electrical engineering field. However, this must be balanced against a positive trend: throughout the 1970s, female labour force participation rates rose, as did rates of female enrolment in formal education. 47/ This is qualified by the fact that women still carry the disproportionate burdens of child-care and other domestic responsibilities. In fact, with rising female labour force participation rates, the total hours of work of women, combining domestic and other work, have, if anything, been rising.

The problem of young migrant workers is a considerable one in Western Europe and North America. 48/ The difficulties that young migrants face are merely a more acute manifestation of those that migrant workers generally encounter. In 1980, the United States had the largest number of economically active foreigners. Many of them were in an irregular situation vis-à-vis their admission, stay, or employment. It was estimated that those economically active foreigners in an irregular situation numbered anything from 2.5 to 4 million persons. With regard to legal migrants, there were about 5 million. Assuming labour force participation to average 50 per cent, there were thus 2.5 million legal migrant workers in the United States in 1980. Two thirds of them came from developing countries. Approximately a half of the irregular migrants are from Mexico. The combined stock, then, of foreigners amounted to some 5 to 6.5 million people. The other North American receiving country, Canada, admitted 63,000 foreign workers for settlement and 74,375 as non-immigrants in 1980. It also extended the authorizations of another 22,889 non-immigrant workers.

In 1980, Western Europe rivalled the United States with a figure of 6.3 million active foreigners (table 25). The Federal Republic of Germany had 2.1 million, France 1.4 million and the United Kingdom nearly 1 million. In addition to the nine countries listed in table 25, five other countries (Denmark, Greece, Italy, Norway and Spain) also host migrant worker populations of about 50,000 each. The number of dependants in all these countries amounts to approximately double the number of recorded active foreigners: the total number of migrants is thus about 13 million. This whole phenomenon of migration has a considerable impact upon the countries concerned, and consequently upon the young people therein. By way of example, in 1978, the flow of migrant workers' savings (remittances) to major migrant-sending countries amounted to $24 billion, and gave these countries an infusion of badly needed hard currency. In the case of a migrant-receiving country, one out of every six motor cars made in the Federal Republic of Germany in 1980 could be attributed to the work of Mediterranean migrants.

Young people among these migrant populations are usually called second-generation migrants. In eight of the nine countries (excluding the United Kingdom) listed in table 25, there were 4.5 million people under 25 years of age of foreign nationality. About 1.5 million of these were economically active. It is not always possible to assess their situation accurately, because of a paucity of data. Some surveys have been conducted, for instance in Belgium and France, to determine whether young migrant workers are in fact leaving the lower working class positions of their parents. These surveys do not provide definitive answers, because they compare the skill levels of fathers and sons, but the measurement of the latter's skill levels only pertains to the early working life.

Table 25. Migrant workers in selected Western European countries, 1980
(Thousands)

Migrant-sending country	Migrant-receiving country									
	Austria	Belgium	France a/	Germany, Federal Republic of	Luxembourg	Nether-lands	Sweden	Switzer-land	United Kingdom b/	Total
Algeria	-	3.2	322.7	1.6	-	-	-	-	-	327.5
Finland	-	-	-	3.7	-	-	108.0	-	1.0	112.7
France	-	38.5	-	54.0	8.5	2.0	7.5	-	14.0	117.2
Greece	-	10.8	3.0	138.4	-	1.2	-	-	6.0	166.9
Italy	-	90.5	146.4	324.3	11.2	12.0	-	301.0	73.0	958.4
Morocco	-	37.3	116.1	16.6	-	33.7	-	-	-	203.7
Portugal	-	6.3	430.6	59.9	13.7	4.2	-	-	5.0	519.7
Spain	-	32.0	157.7	89.3	2.3	10.4	-	85.7	17.0	394.4
Tunisia	-	4.7	65.3	-	-	1.1	-	-	-	71.1
Turkey	28.2	23.0	20.6	623.9	-	53.2	-	20.1	4.0	773.0
Yugoslavia	115.2	3.1	32.2	367.0	0.6	6.6	24.0	62.5	5.0	616.2
Other	31.3	83.2	192.4	490.1	15.6	70.2	94.6	237.0	804.0	2 018.4
Total	174.7	332.6	1 487.0	2 168.8	51.9	194.6	234.1	706.3	929.0	6 279.0

Source: International Labour Organisation, World Labour Report, I (Geneva, 1984).

a/ October 1980, estimate by INSEE on the basis of its 1980 employment survey, which underestimates, by several hundred thousand, categories such as small-scale employers, home-based workers and workers living at construction sites.

b/ May-June 1979, estimate by the Department of Employment on the basis of its 1979 labour force survey.

Second-generation migrants who are born in the migrant-receiving country, or those who enter it prior to compulsory school age, frequently come up to the standard of local young people in their educational and vocational achievements. However, those who enter school at a later age - and there are and will continue to be many of these - encounter enormous difficulties. The most common one is linguistic: their failure to master the local language. There are many special programmes designed to help these disadvantaged young people, but implementation has had to proceed in the teeth of economic austerity. The situation with regard to work is even worse. Second-generation migrants have been disproportionately hit by the unemployment affecting Western Europe, of which young people, as noted above, are generally the chief victims. In France, for example, 26.8 per cent of all unemployed foreign job seekers in 1980 were less than 25 years old. The proportion of young foreign workers in the total migrant labour force was 13.4 per cent, yet those who were unemployed was double of this, 26.8 per cent. In Sweden, the unemployment rate of second-generation migrants was 6.9 per cent, as compared with 3.4 per cent of local youth.

These problems do not exist in the centrally planned economies of Eastern Europe and the USSR. 49/ There are other difficulties here, and these have already been outlined in chapter IV. The most prominent feature of planning in subsequent years is likely to be an emphasis upon increasing the efficiency of the development process. This is a continuation and elaboration of the intensive development strategy which aims at increasing efficiency and quality of production. Such a policy is the result, at least in part, of various difficulties: increasing employment; the limits to investment; the growing problems with raw materials, energy and fuel; and the deteriorating foreign trade position (except in the USSR). Various planned measures have been adopted for the intensive development strategy, some of which have been detailed above. One crucial one is in the direction of better management and planning. Responsibility for plan fulfilment has been shifted down the scale of organizational level. Young people are consequently more closely involved. They are also more responsible, in the sense that there is a tendency to establish closer links between performance and remuneration, though the form this takes differs from country to country.

Notes

1/ "The situation of youth in the Asian and Pacific Region" (SD/RPMIYY/1, 19 May 1983), paper presented to the Regional Preparatory Meeting for the International Youth Year, Bangkok, 26-30 July 1983; "The situation of youth in Europe" (IYY/ECE/RPM/2, 24 June 1983), paper presented to the Regional Preparatory Meeting on International Youth Year, Costinesti, 5-9 September 1983; "The situation and prospects of youth in Latin America" (E/CEPAL/CONF.75/L.2, 5 September 1983), paper presented to the Regional Preparatory Meeting on International Youth Year, San José, 3-7 October 1983; "The situation and needs of youth in Western Asia" (E/ECWA/SDP/W.G.I./3, 1 August 1983), paper presented to the Regional Preparatory Meeting on International Youth Year, Baghdad, 9-13 October 1983. International Youth Year: Regional Plans of Action, 1983 (United Nations publication, 1984).

2/ "The situation of African youth in the 1980s" (ECA/SDEHSD/IYY/83/WD.1, June 1983), paper presented to the Regional Preparatory Meeting for the International Youth Year, Addis Ababa, 20-24 June 1983.

3/ World Economic Survey, 1984, Current Trends and Policies in the World Economy, (United Nations publication, Sales No. E.84.II.C.1), annex.

4/ Food and Agriculture Organization of the United Nations, estimates cited in Inter Press Service, North South News Service (Vienna), No. 063/85, 8 May 1985.

5/ Food and Agriculture Organization of the United Nations, Annual Assessment of the Current World Food Security Situation (Rome, April 1985).

6/ A. K. Sen, Poverty and Famines: An Essay on Entitlement and Deprivation (Oxford, Clarendon Press, 1981).

7/ A. K. Sen, "Development: Which way now?" Economic Journal, No. 93, December 1983, p. 754.

8/ Ibid., p. 760.

9/ Data for this paragraph are drawn from United Nations Educational, Scientific and Cultural Organization, Technical and Vocational Education in the World, 1970-1980: A Statistical Report (Paris, 1983), pp. 13-25.

10/ Excluding Australia, China, Democratic People's Republic of Korea, New Zealand and North America.

11/ Data for this paragraph are drawn from United Nations Educational, Scientific and Cultural Organization, A Summary Statistical Review of Education in the World, 1960-1982, section VI: Drop-out and repetition, pp. 55-59.

12/ 1985 Report on the World Social Situation (United Nations publication, Sales No. E.85.IV.2), p. 26.

13/ "The situation of African youth in the 1980s ...".

14/ "The situation and needs of youth in Western Asia ...".

15/ "Macro-economic data from mid-term review and appraisal of progress in the implementation of the International Development Strategy for the Third United Nations Development Decade in the ECWA Region" (E/ECWA/XI/6, 9 April 1984).

16/ Bahrain, Kuwait, Oman, Qatar, Saudi Arabia and United Arab Emirates.

17/ Egypt, Iraq, Jordan, Lebanon and Syrian Arab Republic.

18/ Democratic Yemen and Yemen.

19/ "Situation and needs of youth in Western Asia...", p. 8.

20/ "Macro-economic data from mid-term review and appraisal ...", p. 19.

21/ "Situation and needs of youth in Western Asia ...", p. 9.

22/ ECOSOC/International Narcotic Control Board/Standing Committee on Estimates/Case Sheets, 1984 for countries mentioned.

23/ "Situation and needs of youth in Western Asia ...".

24/ Ibid., p. 26.

25/ Ibid., pp. 28-29.